THE BOOK OF THE BLESSED VIRGIN

Volume One: Mother of God

THE BOOK OF THE BLESSED VIRGIN
Assembled by F. J. Sheed

VOLUME ONE: MOTHER OF GOD
VOLUME TWO: MOTHER OF MERCY

THE BOOK OF THE SAVIOUR
Assembled by F. J. Sheed

VOLUME ONE: THE INCARNATION
VOLUME TWO: THE PROCLAMATION OF THE KINGDOM
VOLUME THREE: THE PASCHAL MYSTERY

THE BOOK OF THE BLESSED VIRGIN

Volume One: Mother of God

Assembled by F. J. SHEED

CLUNY
Providence, Rhode Island

CLUNY EDITION, 2024

This Cluny edition is a republication, in part, of *The Mary Book*
(Parts I and Part II), originally published by Sheed & Ward, Inc., in 1950.

☞

For more information regarding this title
or any other Cluny Media publication,
please write to info@clunymedia.com, or to
Cluny Media, P.O. Box 1664, Providence, RI 02901

VISIT US ONLINE AT WWW.CLUNYMEDIA.COM

Nihil obstat: Patricius Morris, S.T.D., L.S.S., *Censor Deputatus*

Imprimatur: E. Morrogh Bernard, *Vic. Gen.*
WESTMONASTERII, DIE 16A JUNII 1950

Cover design by Clarke & Clarke
Cover image: Bartolomé Esteban Murillo,
The Adoration of the Shepherds, 1668/1669, oil on canvas
Courtesy of Wikimedia Commons

CONTENTS

F. J. SHEED

⨯ ⨯

ASSEMBLER'S NOTE

written for the original edition of THE MARY BOOK (1950)

In the almost-quarter-century of its existence our firm has published a great many books on Our Lady—naturally, since in the vast conflict of our time we cripple ourselves desperately if we leave her unsummoned. During that same period I have had one experience continually repeated: that, for one aspect of Our Lady's life or operation one book would leap to mind, for another aspect another book, for a third aspect a third book. When I thought of the Immaculate Conception, for instance, I remembered Maurice Zundel's chapter in *Our Lady of Wisdom*: for the profound meaning underlying Our Lady's Sorrows, I had learnt most from Charles Journet's *Our Lady of Sorrows*: for the bearing upon our lives here and now of the period between the Annunciation and Christmas, I would re-read Caryll Houselander's *Reed of God*; for the growth of Catholic devotion to Our Lady, Father Martindale's *Our Blessed Lady* clung in the memory; and so for point after point and book after book.

In other words, each of these books told some part of what is to be known about Our Lady extraordinarily well; if no one of them covered everything, among them they covered a great deal. How much did they

1

cover? I set about finding out. This book is the answer. Practically everything in it comes from books published by us in England or America. The main exceptions are the two prose articles by Jean Guitton [in Volume Two]. I read them in his book *La Vierge Marie* and felt that the book I was assembling simply had to have them. The only authorized translation of *La Vierge Marie* is by A. Gordon Smith, published by Burns, Oates & Washbourne Ltd., London. My thanks are due to them for giving permission to use my own translation because theirs was not ready when *The Mary Book* went to press. I should like to add my own tribute to the excellence of M. Guitton's book.

ANTICIPATION

ↂ ↂ

MOTHER IN ISRAEL

The Old Testament is a collection of singularly masculine documents—I suppose that any oriental literature really is that. Perhaps it is due to this that most of the women mentioned in the literature of the Older Covenant stand out so vividly.

Eve, we need not say, is unique. Mother of All the Living; Mother of all who must die. *Mater pulchrae Spei*—Mother of Fair Hope; then Mother of Tears (so Eastern sailors still invoke her daughter Mary in their long litanies); but Mother, too, of the Promises. The interminable Calvary that seemed destined to Eve's offspring was the hill where should grow that Tree of Salvation, which, as the lovely ancient legend says, was the far-distant offshoot of the Tree of Destruction from which she took the fruit and to Adam gave it and he ate.

Next after Eve came Sara, wife of Abraham. In Genesis 18, we read of the visit of those three mysterious strangers to Abraham, in return for whose hospitality they promised that Sara should bear a son. In a vision, the same promise had been made to Abraham, and he "laughed." How should Sara have a son—she that was ninety years old? Still, he obeyed God's orders, as Zachary, many centuries later, was to do despite initial incredulity. But when Sara overheard the promise made by the strangers she too laughed, wholly disbelieving them, and when she was taxed with her unbelief, was frightened, and denied that she had laughed.... But the months went by, and Isaac was duly born, ancestor of Our Lord according to the flesh.

Alas, that our human sympathies are so often on what turns out to be the "wrong side"! When Isaac was born Sara's mocking laughter was turned into glee: "God hath prepared laughter for me; everyone that heareth will laugh with me!" But no. Agar, Abraham's second wife, but a slave-woman, had already had a son, Ishmael, and Sara refused that the son of the slave should be co-heir with the son of herself, the free. She demanded the expulsion of the slave-woman and her son. Abraham grieved: he loved them. But again God told him not to fear—expel them as he might, the child should grow into a mighty nation. Abraham gave a water-skin to Agar, and turned them adrift in the southern deserts of the land. The water was soon exhausted: she laid her son under a piece of scrub and went and sat down a bow-shot distant, saying: "Ah! Let me not see the child die!" And forthwith she perceived a spring, and revived herself and him, and he became very strong, but a wild man, living in the wilderness, and afterwards he married an Egyptian.

"Ah! Let me not watch the child dying!" On the lips of how many a mother has not that sentence been heard! Saddest is it of all, when the contemplated death is spiritual. When a son "goes wrong." When a father breaks the solemn oaths that he swore when marrying a Catholic wife, and brings a child up deprived of his birthright of the Faith. To us, tragic beyond all else when a Catholic mother has come to feel that "it does not matter very much," and allows her children to slide at ease out of the Church....

Not to look so far forward, we may recall that there is in the world a race of Ishmaels. Pariahs and outcasts. What the poet called "gentlemen rankers"—"damned from here to eternity"—or, indeed, men in no social sense "gentlemen"—"rankers" if they are able so much as to get into *any* "rank"—often quite isolated, true Ishmaels, their hand against every man's and every man's hand against them. Ah! If but one might be privileged to know even one such—to be his friend unshakenly; to endure, even, his dying without apparent faith and certainly without sacraments or any sort of act (to human eye) of faith and of contrition, and yet to be able to affirm to God that one had tied up one's heart and life with him, and that apart from his salvation heaven itself would hardly be worth having—well, one would be talking nonsense; but it would be a nonsense talked both by Moses and St. Paul; it would be a way of laying down one's own life for the sheep—only, our Lord made it quite clear that such a laying down of life would be the supreme form of finding it, one's own life, and the life of my Ishmael.

The generations passed: idyllic stories are to be read, like that especially of the wooing of Rebekah, the pastoral charm of which is hardly to be surpassed: she became the mother of the twins, Jacob and Esau. Here again the promises of God passed through Jacob, who twice so disgustingly cheated Esau: and did so the second time at the instigation of Rebekah herself. Making every allowance for the oriental delight in duplicity, we have to say that the stories are ugly; we acknowledge that God can, and often does, make use of very imperfect instruments; Esau went off to the descendants of Ishmael and took a wife from among them; Jacob married Rachel, who could not shake off her ancestral paganism, and has but little "personality" in her story; and since it is not the story of Jacob that we are recalling, we leave her shadowy figure to melt into the distant dazzle of oriental sunlight.

No other Hebrew woman now emerges from that earlier dazzle save her whom we prefer to name Miriam—for who, save one, in that long history must be called "Mary"? Despite the "Magdalen," for whom we keep *that* name. She was the sister of Moses, and undoubtedly a leader among the women of Israel during its escape from Egypt. She clashed her cymbals—she led the triumph song—but afterwards she, too, was disloyal, and was struck with leprosy. She was healed, and had a "future" in Hebrew memories, but on the whole, I think, for her brother's sake.

Moses died, having seen the Promised Land from the top of Mount Nebo, but he did not enter it.

In the troubled times of the entering of the Hebrews, startling as it may seem to us, the only woman's name that we care to retain is that of Rahab, the courtesan of Jericho, who saved the lives of Josue's two spies, and so, speaking humanwise, of the whole people. The red cord was bound around her windowbars, and her entire household was exempted in the sacking of the city. But Josue, too, died, and a period of all but chaos followed. There was no law: every man "did that which was right in his own eyes." Here and there local personalities arose, who "judged" the people and exercised brief and local authority. Of these, strange as it may seem, one was Debora (Judges 4). "She judged Israel at that time...the children of Israel came up to her for judgment." When the soldier Barak was told to advance against Sisera, he refused to go unless she came with him. She promised that she would: "nevertheless the journey shall not be for thine honour." For the Lord would give Sisera into the hands of a woman. This woman was Jael, who cajoled the exhausted Sisera into her tent, sent him to sleep, and drove a tent-peg completely through his skull. Concerning this event Debora sang a psalm which may be almost the oldest piece of Hebrew poetry that has come down to us. "The rulers ceased in Israel—they ceased—until I, I, Debora, arose—till I arose, a Mother in Israel!"

This story is savage; the hymn is superb; with such reverses, and slow, slow advances, did the History of God for the Hebrews proceed.

As though to refresh us, during this very period occurred the romance of Ruth. A man from Bethlehem of Juda had gone with his wife Naomi into the land of Moab, where the savage Kemosh was worshipped. His two sons married Moabite women—Orpa and Ruth. All three men died. Naomi resolved to return to her own land[1]; and of her two daughters-in-law, though Naomi begged them both to leave her and stay in their own land, Ruth chose to go with her. The Scriptures have bequeathed to our language, as a treasure for ever, her exquisite chant:

Entreat me not to leave thee
Nor to return from following after thee:
For whither thou goest, I will go;
And where thou lodgest, I will lodge:
Thy people shall be my people,
And thy God, my God!
Where thou diest, I will die,
And there will I be buried—
The Lord do so to me, and more also,
If aught but Death separate thee and me!

---

1. We are apt to forget how small was the scene of the Palestinian drama. Naomi had only about thirty miles to go; and Bethlehem could be seen from the mountains of Moab.

It is this part of the story which has made it immortal, though the rest is full of interesting Israelite customs and romance. In the end Ruth married her kinsman Boaz, and became the grandmother of King David.

But before that had occurred the episode of Samuel, which begins with the pathetic history of his mother Anna, who at first could have no child. She went year by year to Silo, where the Ark was, and prayed with such desperate earnestness to be freed from this "disgrace," that the chief priest, Eli, who was watching her lips move, thought that she was drunken and bade her leave the House of God. "Nay, my lord," she said: "but I am a woman of a sorrowful spirit: neither wine nor strong drink have I drunk; but I was pouring out my soul before the Lord!" He bade her go in peace; and in due course Samuel was born. In 1 Kings 2, her song of thanksgiving is related. None can help comparing it with the Magnificat. Whole verses are similar. Yet what a difference! Both poems must be read throughout, if we are to savour that. Our Lady's is as Jewish as possible—traditional in phrasing, exultant, thrilling with praise and gratitude: yet how gentle, how sweet, how without any taste of rancour or triumphing over critics and the scornful! But you cannot help feeling precisely *that* in the earlier psalm, late though it may have been when the traditional words were actually written down. The later this was done, the nearer the time of Mary, the deeper the gulf is cleft between all the hymns (and the Magnificat in particular) handed down by St. Luke, and these Old Testament paeans.

I cannot bring myself to find beauty in any of the stories of women to be read in the remainder of the Old Testament. Assuredly there is romance in those of the women who helped Elias and Eliseus; and that of Bathsheba is of extreme pathos; she, too, was an ancestress of our Lord: St. Matthew in his genealogy names her curtly "Uriah's wife"; St. Luke, quite uncharacteristically, omits all names of women in *his* genealogy.[2] But after this, the brief incidents, where women are concerned, are not attractive[3]; the episode of Jezabel is grim and dramatic—it, too, has left ineffaceable marks upon our language. And to *our* taste, that of the heroine "Judith" (let alone Susanna) is unpleasant.

No doubt Psalm 44 introduces the almost hierarchic figure of the Princess whose marriage hymn it partly is: no doubt the splendour of her robes is dwelt upon—but all this is rather to exhort her to "forget thy people and thy father's house," and to look forward to children, rather than back to the home of her girlhood. Nor can we doubt but that the Jews saw a symbolical religious value in the "Canticle," else it would never have found its way into their Canon. But the symbolism is obscure.

There are, of course, not a few references to "good women" and their value, up and down the Old Testament; and the famous passage in Proverbs where the idea is much expanded; otherwise I can think of nothing save the great prophecies of Micheas 5:2–5, and Isaias 7, obscure though these be, unless, I think, we accustom ourselves to the "prophetic vision," which included one thing within another—depth upon depth of meaning; width beyond width of horizon.

Thus Micheas was envisaging the sack of Samaria and the deportation of its citizens by Assyria. He wished to say that this devastation should not last for ever, but only until from Bethlehem should come

---

2. The place of Thamar, who sinned with Juda, in Our Lord's ancestry, has often been commented on; but she remains without distinct personality.

3. The Queen of Saba, visiting Solomon, has bequeathed to us two sentences, "The half was not told me," and, "There was no more spirit left in her"—but how vulgar, if I may say so, she remains!

forth God's ruler for the People, one whose goings-forth (origin) were from of old, yes, from ancient days. When she, who was destined to bear him, should do so, then would victory be assured, and the scattered people return. It is not difficult to argue that the prophet meant, at first, that from David's city should come forth one of David's ancient stock, a military leader who should restore freedom and unity to Israel—all under divine Providence. And were one to attend only to the beginning and the end of this passage, where attention is so definitely concentrated on the Assyrian enemy, it would be harder to suppose that the prophet meant more than that, than to confine his meaning within just those limits. But so high does his inspiration rise between these earlier and later texts that you can be sure that he was contemplating also the true Messias, as it were shining forth *through* the immediate conqueror, and spreading his rays much further than he.[4]

There is little if anything that can count as "Catholic tradition" about these words. It is quite otherwise with the prophecy in Isaias. Here Achaz, king of Juda, was seeking to make an alliance with the pagan empire of Assyria in view of the attack made on him by the kings of Damascus (Syria) and of Israel (the northern kingdom). This meant inviting the pagan into God's land, and trusting to man rather than God, and deliberately making the Chosen People into a state vassal to the pagan. Isaias rebuked, yet encouraged him, and offered him any "sign," however amazing, that he might choose, as proof that the unholy alliance was not needed for his rescue. Contemptuous, despondent, or just unbelieving, Achaz refused. Indignantly Isaias said that God Himself would then

---

4.   I think everyone recognises that this passage is Messianic—it may actually *allude* to Isaias 7.

provide a sign. Let but the Maiden now conceive and bear a son—and before the boy were of age to discern good from evil, the land would be desolate, and he would be living a life of all but destitution. Egypt and Assyria alike would devastate all Palestine—as indeed they did during the next reign. Yet should that devastation not be everlasting—for the boy should be called Immanu-El: "God (is) with us," and as God's agent should deliver the land.

We must remember that a "sign" need not mean something physically obvious or immediately intelligible, let alone some startling prodigy such as had been offered to and refused by Achaz. It could be something that might be recalled and interpreted only when what it foreshadowed had occurred, and *because* it occurred. Thus, what our Lord said about the destruction of the Temple and its rebuilding, the disciples did not fathom till after the Resurrection; so Achaz may have taken these words merely on their face value. Should a maiden now conceive and bear a son, before his boyhood should be over, Egypt and Assyria would have devastated Palestine. Nor is there anything essentially, intrinsically, Messianic (let alone incarnational) in the name Immanuel.[5]

There is, however, the disconcerting fact that Isaias does not say "a maiden," but "*the* maiden." It is, to my mind, perfectly impossible to see in this a reference either to Achaz's wife or to Isaias's, nor can any other definite "maiden" be suggested as alluded to. I certainly think that the prophet meant, directly, that should the destined maiden, mother of

---

5. It is, I think, admitted now by all that the word translated "virgin" is rightly so translated. Not all, however, would see in the words, as such, a prophecy of a virgin birth. If I say: "The blind shall see," I mean that those who now are blind shall see, having by that very fact ceased to be blind. Nor indeed is Isaias here insisting on the virgin birth of the Rescuer: he is announcing dates and times, "that when it shall come to pass you may remember that I have told you" (John 16:9).

the promised Messias, *now* conceive and bear her son, the land would be devastated before he was grown up. But from the outset, within this, he sees the Messianic history of the People, and similarly, even when he speaks of his own son—before *he* could so much as speak, the devastation should have occurred. But into such splendours of vision and diction does he forthwith ascend as to leave no doubt that his state of mind through this great section is prophetic, that he envisages the ultimate and actual Messias, and indeed, his transcendent relationship with God. The Church, since the Christian revelation of the Incarnation and the Virgin Birth, has consistently seen in this passage a true prophecy of both. Hebrew prophecy must then be acknowledged as constantly disconcerting a modern reader, especially one trained in the rigorous methods of Greek philosophy, of Latin explicit and legalized formulas, and even of ordinary English, which likes to "say what it has got to say" as simply and straightforwardly as possible. The divine Sun peers through the clouds of human Hebrew thought, shoots forth a ray, withdraws itself, reappears through a different rift in the tumultuous swirling vapours, and leaves us hesitating as to what exactly we have seen. The moment you think you have reached the eternal and infinite plane, you are distracted by allusions to ancient wars between long-ago dead empires: and, when your mind is fixed on these, the prophetic vision suddenly opens out and such marvellous things are written that you know yourself in a world into which no other literature admits you. Only under the full Christian light can the history of the Hebrews—a substantial enduring "prophecy" in itself—be properly understood. Isaias is to me unintelligible unless I affirm that in these passages his mind went also, and after a while chiefly if not wholly, to the Messias who should come, he knew not when, born truly of a mother, he knew not whom, and should effect a rescue far transcending the defeat merely of this king or that, or of any passing Empire.

Was the vision of the Mother of the Messias habitually before the eyes of the Hebrew people, or even of their prophets? We can hardly think so; nor, certainly, the idea that she should be a virgin-mother. Much later on, vague suggestions floated about in rabbinic literature to the effect that his birth would be somehow extraordinary: "When Messias cometh, no man knoweth whence he is" (John 7:27–28); but this refers not only to immediate ancestry or parentage, but also to place of origin. Not only Eve, but Adam, seem to drop almost wholly out of Hebrew imagination and literature, unlike Abraham, Moses, Samuel, David and quite subordinate personages, like Dathan. Perhaps this is because the attention of the national mind was concentrated rather on the future than on the past—this is one point in which Hebrew religion differed so much from other religions that surrounded it—they put the Golden Age in the past. All, Our Lady herself, normally expected the Rescuer to be born of human wedlock. Anyhow, we have seen that despite a few notable figures—national heroines on the whole—the divine process leaps straight from Eve to Mary, and it is on this transcendent vision of the Woman, ever present in God's plan, and actively sharing in the working-out of his purpose, that St. John, in the very last book of the Bible, will fix his eye.

ఞ ఞ

ESTHER AS TYPE OF OUR LADY

The promises made by Almighty God to his chosen people were, so far as the material part of them was concerned, conditional promises. The coming of the Messiah was an absolute promise; it was part of the fore-ordained purpose of God. But that the people of Israel should live secure from foreign aggression, that they should have dominion over their neighbours, that they should possess in perpetuity the fertile land of Chanaan—all that was conditional upon their own actions. I will be to them a God, and they shall be to me a people—if the Jews ceased to recognize the unique majesty of Almighty God, if they fell into idolatry, and worshipped other gods besides him, then the covenant was retracted, and he was no longer pledged to protect or to redeem them. Again and again this situation arose, until finally, some seven hundred years before the beginning of our era, foreign conquerors took captive first the ten apostate tribes and then the true Jews of Juda, and carried them all away to the East, where they lived in exile for nearly two centuries.

God utilizes our faults; it was not without his intent that his people thus became scattered among the nations. For he knew that, as long as they dwelt in their own country and held closely to their own home life, the Jews would be the last people on earth to exercise a missionary influence, and so prepare the way for the preaching of his gospel. "For this reason," says the canticle of Tobias, "hath he dispersed you among the nations who know him not, that you may tell forth his marvellous works, and make them to know that there is no other God Almighty, save him alone." In order that our Lord's crucifixion in an obscure province at one corner of the Roman Empire might have a world-wide repercussion in its influence on men's hearts, it was necessary that the world should be sprinkled with little colonies of Jewish citizens, keeping alive their own national traditions and yet in touch, to a certain extent, with their Gentile neighbours. That end was secured by the captivity. But it was secured not without difficulty, not without ill-feeling. The Jews have no instinct of colonization; they neither impose on others a culture of their own, nor acclimatize themselves perfectly as the citizens of an alien kingdom. Their stubborn independence, which is their chief religious virtue, is their chief political drawback. And accordingly, not once nor twice in the world's history, the Jewish people has been threatened with extinction by neighbours piqued at the insularity of its outlook, and jealous of its commercial success.

One of these crises happened, it would seem, at a time, not certainly identified, when the whole Eastern world lay under the dominion of Persia. Under the reign of Assuerus, a plot had been hatched against the Jews by their enemies, and all preparations had been made for a pogrom which was to cover the whole extent of the Persian empire. The facts were public; the Jewish people was in mourning, its adversaries triumphant. In that crisis, two influences saved God's people from destruction. A Jew, Mardochaeus, had preserved the king's life by giving timely information of a plot laid against him; and his name had been enrolled, according to Persian custom, among those who were described as "the King's benefactors." And his niece, Esther, had pleased the king by her beauty, and had been publicly acclaimed as his queen. But there was a difficulty to be overcome. The good service Mardochaeus had done was, it is true, on record, but he had no means of recalling it to the king's memory.

No means, unless his niece Esther would act for him; and she, in her turn, was cramped by the etiquette of the Court. It was not lawful for her to enter the royal presence unless she were summoned to it; and the penalty for a breach of this ordinance was death. Esther, vanquishing her own fears for the sake of her fellow-countrymen, made bold to enter the presence unbidden. She received a royal welcome: "What is the matter, Esther? I am thy brother, fear not; thou shalt not die, for this law is not made for thee, but for all others." So she obtained her audience and won her suit; and the Jews, instead of being massacred, were in a position to take vengeance on their persecutors.

Why am I telling you this story? From other incidents in the Old Testament, however crude their atmosphere, however primitive their setting, it may be possible for us to derive moral exhortation. But these intrigues of the harem, these tales of plot and counterplot in the corrupt politics of an oriental despotism—what message have they for us, what instruction can they convey? I am only choosing this story out of a dozen others I might have chosen, to illustrate the principle, familiar to Christian piety, that there is a mystical significance in the Old Testament everywhere; and that, above all, the history of the Jewish people foreshadows and typifies the glories of our Blessed Lady. The Old Testament is, largely, a record of barbarian times; blood flows freely in its chronicles, and there is treachery, and violence, and lust, and crafty revenge;

there are dull passages, too, long lists of names, and prescriptions about ceremonial ordinances which have ceased to have any interest for us; there are interminable moral precepts, and prophecies baffling in their obscurity. But through this tangled skein runs a single golden thread; between these soiled pages lies, now and again, a pressed flower that has lost neither its colour nor its sweetness. That thread, that flower, is the mention, by type and analogue, of her whom all generations of Christendom have called blessed, the Virgin of Virgins, the Queen of Heaven, the holy Mother of God.

It is not wonderful that it should be so. For our Lady is, after all, the culmination of that long process of selection, of choosing here and rejecting there a human instrument suited to his purpose, which is so characteristic of God's dealings with his ancient people. I think we can observe, throughout the whole of that process, two principles at work. One is, that God chooses, every now and again, the unlikely candidate, the one we should not have chosen; chooses the younger son rather than the elder, the despised character rather than the prominent character. You see, he will shew us that grace is free; that his choice falls upon this human instrument or that, without any antecedent merits on their part to account for it. And at the same time, he proves that his choice was justified; as the history of their dealings unfolds itself, we realize that the unlikely candidate was the right candidate, corresponds with the grace given and, not under compulsion but with free election of the will, seconds God's purposes and proves a ready accomplice for his salutary design. God's grace and man's free will corresponding with it—that ancient mystery is illustrated at every turn of the Old Testament story, until at last we turn over the page into the New Testament and find its ideal illustration in the life of Our Lady herself.

The promises were made to Abraham's seed—nothing was said about his wife Sarah; was it impossible, then, that an illegitimate child should inherit? Here is Ishmael, a sturdy son of the desert; will he not suffice for God's purposes, since Sarah is barren? Oh, that Ishmael might live before thee! But no; we must allow God to do things in his own way; Ishmael is rejected, and the promise is not fulfilled until, out of due time, in the extreme old age of his parents, Isaac is born. Isaac again has two sons, this time both legitimate sons, yet here again the selective process is at work. Even before the children are born it is prophesied that the elder shall serve the younger. And so it is; Jacob is chosen, not the world's candidate, not the more vigorous character, to all outward appearance, and yet the choice is justified. Jacob has twelve sons; on whom will the choice fall? On Reuben, the eldest? No, unstable as water, he shall not excel; no, not on him. On Benjamin, then, the youngest, his father's darling, the child of the beloved Rachel? No, not on him. On Joseph, surely, the boy who was sold into slavery and became the governor of all Egypt—he, surely, is pointed out by his career as the ancestor of the Messiah? No, the choice is not to fall on him. It is the treacherous, bloodthirsty Juda who is selected this time—a choice that was justified when his descendants conquered the most difficult and most secure fastnesses of the Chanaanitish country. A king is appointed, and he comes of the tribe of Benjamin; is this, then, to be a reversal of God's plan that royalty should belong to the tribe of Juda? No, God allows him to lead his people for a time to victory, but only for a time; this is not the man after God's own heart. At last a man is found after God's own heart, the son of Jesse in Bethlehem of Juda; but once more it is not the likely candidate. Jesse's eldest son, Eliab, appears before the prophet Samuel, who supposes at once that this is the Lord's anointed; but no, we are not to look on his countenance, nor on the height of his stature, because God has rejected him. Seven sons of Jesse pass before Samuel, and still the horn of oil has not done its work. Is there no other? Yes, there is a young one; a mere boy, who has been left to look after the sheep. So David is brought in: and the Lord said, Arise, and anoint him, for this is he. And among David's sons, too, it was not Absalom or Adonias, princes who could lead a people into rebellion; it was the peaceful Solomon on whom the lot of the kingdom fell. Always God sees the human agent he wants, and makes him what he wants him to be.

In what, then, does all this long, careful process of selection culminate? By two separate streams the blood of David came down to Zorobabel, the hero of Israel's return from captivity. After that, it will have crossed and recrossed; we cannot even tell for certain the name of St. Joseph's father. Nor do we know in what degree of relationship St. Joseph stood to our Blessed Lady. We only know that somehow, through cadet branches, that royal lineage came down to the second Eve, and the cycle of Old Testament history was complete. To what had the divine promises looked forward? To David, the man after God's own heart? To Solomon, the wisest of all princes? To Zorobabel, the deliverer of his people? No, to one village girl, a shepherd's daughter and a carpenter's bride. She is the culmination of all that process; for in her human nature reached to its highest dignity, to greet the divine condescension of the Incarnate. In her, as nowhere else, God had found the human instrument suited to his purpose; the worthy receptacle of a grace that had not dwelt on earth since Adam lost his paradise. The work of selection is consummated; mankind stands ready for its Redeemer.

And, as she is the culmination of the Old Testament, so Christian devotion has found in the Old Testament titles and symbols everywhere that can be referred to her. She is the second Eve; in her the serpent's head is crushed. She is the new Ark of our salvation, ready to re-people the world with the seed of grace. She is Jacob's ladder, by which our prayers go up, and graces come down upon us in return. Her Virginity is the bush Moses saw in the desert, burning ever, yet never consumed. She is the ark of the new covenant, where God keeps tryst with man; she is Aaron's rod—the single bloom of innocence that sprang from our corrupt nature. As Rahab betrayed Jericho to Josue, so through her Jesus our Saviour entered the rebellious citadel of man's heart. She is Gedeon's fleece, wet with the dew of heaven while all the ground was dry. She is the king's daughter, of whom David sang, and the faithful Sulamite of the Canticles, and Respha the daughter of Aia, weeping for her sons that were crucified. She is the Rod of Jesse, and the well of living waters, and the gate shut up, save for the prince. Daughter and Crown of the Old Testament, what wonder if patriarchs, and kings, and prophets spoke of her?

On the feast of her birthday, the gospel is a long string of names, all the names of those ancestors she shared with St. Joseph. Do you ever wonder, as they are read, why we should pay so much attention to them—Aram begetting Aminadab, and Aminadab begetting Naasson, and Naasson begetting Salmon? Well, of course, it is appropriate that St. Matthew should begin in that way. We may find it sticky reading, but it is this sticky page which joins the New Testament on to the Old. But for myself I like to think of this long list of names as a list of the names our Blessed Lady *forgot*. "Harken, O daughter, and consider, and incline thy ear; *forget* also thy own kindred, and thy father's house." When we think of St. Joachim's household, we must remember that it was a family which had come down in the world. We saw David, the shepherd boy, raised up to be King of Israel, and now we see St. Joachim, descended from so many kings, brought low again and taking up the calling of a shepherd—back at the old trade. Very often, if you meet some member of a family which has come down in the world, you will find that he, or more probably she, is apt to think a good deal about those important ancestors who enjoyed the family fortunes; there will be books containing the family history; there will be books containing family trees, and the pathetic little drawing-room will be decorated with prints of the portraits by Kneller and Romney that were sold long ago. Was our Lady like that? They had called her Mariam, and they probably thought that the name meant "Princess." I know the scholars say it does not, but St. Joachim, probably, was not much of a scholar. Did he, perhaps, choose this popular name, which comes in the pedigree of the Herods about the same time, with a sort of holy irony, to remind himself and his neighbours of the height from which the family had fallen?

Our Lady was not like that. We know, from her own words, what she thought about it all. Surely that is the point of the verse, "He has put down the mighty from their seat, and exalted the lowly." What have the mighty got to do with it (we naturally ask)? Why, surely our Lady is referring to those ancestors of hers, who had once been kings. It would have passed almost without comment, if God had chosen a princess to be the Mother of Christ. How much more impressive, that he should have put down the mighty line of David from its royal throne, and then have chosen a descendant of theirs, born in a shepherd's cottage, to be the Queen of Heaven! No, our Lady did not waste her time in meditating on the glories of the past, like those people we were talking about. She was, if I may dare to put it that way, so splendidly sensible: knew so well how to make the best of things. We know that our Blessed Lord was born in a stable. How do we know that? St. Luke does not say so; you will not find the word "stable" in the New Testament at all. No, the fact comes out (as it were), inadvertently; "she brought forth a son, her first-born, and laid him in a manger, because there was no room for them in the inn." Can't you *hear* our Lady saying that? "Unfortunately there was no room in the inn; so I had to put him in a manger," as if it were the most obvious thing in the world.

WE VALUE, then, this story of Mardochaeus and Esther because we find in it a type of our Lady's position in the economy of grace. How often a face or a scene arrests us, only because it bears some resemblance to a face or a scene we love! So it is with these Old Testament figures; they borrow their interest from the future. Like the people of the Jews, the Church of God has its enemies and its detractors; its peace is continually threatened by the world's hatred for its strictness of principle. And when times of trouble come upon us, we, too, would win a royal audience; we would ask redress for our grievances from the King of Kings. As the Jews could plead on their own behalf the loyal act of Mardochaeus, so we would plead before God, our one hope of pardon, the all-sufficient sacrifice of his Son. But who will plead it for us? It is not that we distrust his goodness; but, conscious of our need and of our own unworthiness, we would find some advocate who has a better claim on his attention than ourselves. Who has a better right to stand in God's royal presence than our Blessed Lady? The law which included us all under the curse of original sin was a law made for all others, but not for her. Who else dare touch the sceptre that sways a universe?

And if the Church, rich in the merits of so many saints, still has recourse first of all to her, still prefixes her name to every solemn invocation, what of ourselves, so unventuresome in our faith, so conscious of weakness and of past failure? Shall we not too call her in as an advocate for our private needs, however little their importance? The Queen of Heaven, yet she is a woman, of the same fashioning as ourselves. We say to her, as Mardochaeus said to Esther, "Remember the days of thy low estate; and do thou speak to the king for us, and deliver us from death." We have all of us this instinct about our Blessed Lady, that she is not merely the Mother of all our fallen race, but the Mother of each individually; not *our* Mother, but *my* Mother. Protestants sometimes laugh at us because we address ourselves, now to our Lady of Perpetual Succour, now to our Lady of Good Counsel, now to our Lady of Lourdes, and so on, as if they were so many different people. But the case is much worse than that, if they only knew; every individual Catholic has a separate our Lady to pray to, his Mother, the one who seems to care for him individually, has won him so many favours, has stood by him in so many difficulties, as if she had no other thought or business in heaven but to watch over him.

Let us commit to her, then, the outcome of this retreat, entrust to her keeping whatever lights and graces we have received in the course of it, as children hand over to their mother some coin that has been given to them, because they know they would only lose it if they tried to keep it for themselves. We shall forget, sometimes, to pray for this or that grace, according to our resolutions; she will not forget to offer the petition for us, if we will take it to her now. Let us say the *Salve Regina* in her honour, meditating it to ourselves as we go.

Hail, holy Queen—crowned in heaven by the piety of your ascended Son, crowned on earth by the gratitude of a million suppliants. How little you regarded your royal lineage as a daughter of the house of David! "Harken, O daughter, and consider, incline thy ear, and forget thy people and thy father's house: instead of thy fathers thou shalt have children, whom thou mayest make princes in all lands"—you are crowned, not by some accident of birth, for the sake of those who went before you, but by the loving homage of all those saints who derive from you their spiritual succession. Hail, holy Queen, still remembering in the courts of heaven your low estate, the anxieties of womanhood and the simple cares of home!

Mother of Mercy—if it be true that we inherit from our parents not our bodily features only, but something also of the stuff of our minds, the make-up of our temperaments, then he, whose sacred Humanity was perfectly human, must have received from you some gift of human tenderness. At least, as his Mother, you brought into the world Incarnate Mercy; at least, by your own compassion, you have won the title *Mater Misericordiae!*

Hail, our Life, our Sweetness, and our Hope—our Life, because we owe all our supernatural activities to our incorporation into him, who lay in your womb and was nursed at your breast; our Sweetness, because there are times of melancholy and spiritual dullness when nothing will throw a ray of light across our minds except the thought of a trusted friend; and, of all the friends we have, none is more trusted, none dwells in the memory more gratefully, than you; our Hope, because life has its shadows ahead of us, and the shadow of death lies behind those, and beyond death itself, terrors still more formidable, unless you will relieve our cares, brighten our death-beds, and safeguard our passage into eternity.

To thee do we cry, poor banished children of Eve—there is a duality of purpose in us, that still spoils our best aspirations and betrays our highest resolutions. Victims of a baffled hope and an unsatisfied desire, we, Eve's children, carry in our troubled foreheads the sentence of our exile; we cannot find ourselves here. But you knew nothing of that mortal weakness, that divided purpose; Eve's daughter; inheriting from her what no other daughter of hers ever inherited, her innocence, you replaced her and made atonement for her fault, God's perfect creature of woman as God meant woman to be.

To thee do we send up our sighs, mourning and weeping in this vale of tears—God has given us in our mortal lives so much that is gracious, so much that is comforting, the beauty of storm and sunset, books and music, and the love of friends and the smiles of children; and yet, how few steps we take on our daily path without meeting some disappointment in our own lives, some tragedy in the lives of others! All this reminds us of our fallen state; earth's joys may suffice us for the moment, but in time of trouble we fly for consolation to you.

Turn then, most gracious Advocate, thine eyes of mercy towards us—we see you pictured, standing by the Crucifix, with all your eyes and all your soul directed upwards in compassionate regard towards him who hangs there. But let us not think of you as turning away your eyes from earth, away from the tragedies of human sorrow and the crucifixions of human injustice; rather, look upon all these, and then turn back your eyes, troubled with compassion for our human misfortune, to him.

And after this our exile, shew unto us the blessed Fruit of thy womb, Jesus—we see you again, bending over the manger at Bethlehem, uniting in one ecstasy of love the pride of a Mother with the adoration of a Creature. He who dwells in heaven, the first-born of all creation, came down to earth and was a Child for our sakes; we in our turn, children of earth, pray that we may be exalted to the joys of heaven; through the merits you won for us by sharing his Calvary on earth, we hope, in heaven, to share your Bethlehem with you.

O clement, O loving, O sweet Virgin Mary! Holy Mary, Mother of God, pray for us sinners now and at the hour of our death.

ADAM LAY IBOUNDEN

Adam lay ibounden,
bounden in a bond
  four thousand winters
thought he not too long;
  and all was for an apple,
an apple that he took,
  as clerkès finden
written in their book.

ne had the apple taken been,
  the apple taken been,
ne had never our lady
  been Heaven's queen.
blessed be the time
  that apple taken was!
therefore we may singen
  Deo gracias.

FROM THE ANNUNCIATION
TO THE ASSUMPTION

⌁

VINCENT MCNABB, O.P.

꒜ ꒜

THE ANNUNCIATION

There is a state of mind which is greatly moved by the absence of certain doctrines from all or some books of the New Testament. Thus, to one who finds no explicit mention of Mary the mother of Jesus in any of the Epistles of St. Paul, the Catholic devotion to Mary the mother of Jesus, that devotion which is common to West and East, seems almost sacrilegious.

This perplexed state of mind is met by a general and a particular argument. The general argument is taken from the fragmentary and—if we may so call it—casual nature of the contents of the New Testament. The particular argument is based on showing that the writer whose epistles seem to ignore the unique dignity of Our Blessed Lady has elsewhere shown that in this doctrine, as in all other doctrines, he is in line with the Catholic tradition of East and West.

This particular argument is of avail for those who find with bewilderment that not one word about the office and dignity of the mother of Jesus is to be found in the two weighty epistles of Peter. Their bewilderment should be at an end when they realise that the doctrine of the Virgin Birth and therefore of the divine maternity of Mary is wrought into the Gospel of St. Mark, which is in substance the authentic teaching of St. Peter.

Still greater bewilderment of mind is likely to be caused by the entire absence of direct mention of the Virgin Mother of Jesus in the epistles of St. Paul (though we recall Gal. 4:4, "God sent his Son made of a woman"). If we include the Epistle to the Hebrews, which even by all non-Catholic exegetes is admitted to be Pauline in its doctrine if not in its style, St. Paul's writings not only rival in bulk the four gospels, but they far exceed in bulk the rest of the New Testament. They are written to almost every class and grouping of the early Church. Moreover, as in bulk they can compare with the gospels, so too, their publication on the one side probably preceded the earliest gospel and on the other side almost synchronized with the latest synoptic gospel. Lastly, these lengthy, wide-aimed epistles, extending over a long period of years, extend also over such a wide range of doctrine, and treat that doctrine with such fullness of exposition, that some modern critics have looked upon Paul of Tarsus and not Jesus of Nazareth as the effective maker of the Faith, if not of the Church. Yet from all that mass of closely-reasoned doctrine for "Gentile and Jew, barbarian and Scythian, bond and free" we cannot extract one direct mention of Mary, the Virgin Mother of Jesus Christ!

We have pointed out that to such a difficulty as this absence of all mention of our Lady in the epistles of St. Peter there are two answers— the general and the particular. For the more scholarly minds the general answer may be sufficient. Such minds realise that though St. Paul wrote on many subjects, yet he could not write on all, even if he had wished, as assuredly he did not wish, to give the early Church a "Catechism of Christian Doctrine."

Yet happily not only scholarship but simple faith is ministered to in the New Testament. The general answer to the difficulty is accompanied and strengthened by the particular answer. The difficulty of St. Paul's fourteen epistles is met by the Gospel and the Acts of St. Luke, which are in substance the teaching of St. Paul. Too much stress can hardly be laid on the obvious fact that St. Luke, the companion and, as we should say, the secretary of St. Paul, would not publish works of such primary importance as the *Gospel* and the *Acts* without consulting his master St. Paul. We may be excused for further labouring a plain truth now accepted by sound biblical criticism. This truth may be formulated by saying that St. Luke's Gospel and Acts of the Apostles are no less Pauline in doctrine than the Epistle to the Hebrews.

(a) The chief witness of Luke like the chief witness of Matthew is contained in the first two chapters.

We confess that we know no *a priori* arguments against the possibility that St. Joseph was responsible for the first two chapters of Matthew and that Mary, the wife of Joseph, was responsible for the first two chapters of Luke.

Moreover, on any theory of the person of Jesus Christ this view of the opening chapters of Luke would seem not merely possible but even probable. Only two theories can be broached: either that Jesus Christ was born of a Virgin, or that Jesus Christ was not born of a Virgin. But in neither case could the (true or false) doctrine of the Virgin Birth arise contemporaneously without the active co-operation of the alleged virgin mother. Those who deny that Mary, though mother, was a virgin mother would see how likely it is that the whole story of a miraculous conception would naturally come from the imposter herself. On the other hand, those of us who hold the doctrine of the Virgin Birth must see that the story of the miraculous conception must come from the mother and from her alone. Thus both defenders and opponents of the Virgin Birth will agree that it is not only possibly but probably the account of no other than the Mother of Jesus which we possess in the opening chapters of St. Luke's Gospel.

(b) Confirmation of this view is to be found in the Hebrew character of these two chapters. St. Luke's Gospel, directed as it was by St. Paul, the Doctor of the Gentiles, was meant not for a Jewish but for a Gentile audience. We may, therefore, describe the opening chapters as a Jewish or Hebrew prologue to a Greek Gospel.

(c) St. Matthew's text reads, "Entering into the house they found the child with Mary his mother" (Matt. 2:11). There is no mention of Joseph. But St. Luke's text describing the coming of the shepherds reads, "They found Mary and Joseph and the infant" (Luke 2:16). St. Joseph is not only mentioned, but mentioned in the place of honour next to the child Jesus.

Moreover we have the phrase "his parents." Thus, "When *his parents* brought in the child Jesus" (Luke 2:27). Again, "His *parents* went every year to Jerusalem" (Luke 2:41). Again, "The child Jesus remained in Jerusalem. And *his parents* knew it not" (Luke 2:43). This phrase is made the stronger by the account of the finding in the Temple, in which our Lady says to her child Jesus "Behold thy father and I have sought thee sorrowing" (Luke 2:48). This is the strongest argument against the Virgin Birth to be found in the four gospels. But it is the exaltation of the dignity of Joseph, the foster-father of Jesus. Coming as it does in the second chapter of St. Luke's Gospel, it serves to confirm our view that these chapters are due to the pen or dictation of the Virgin wife who recognised in her husband the God-appointed head or "father" of the Holy

Family. We believe that no literary artist, but only a mother, could have fallen upon this phrase. Few phrases are more commonly on the lips of a mother when commanding or entreating a child than "Your father is displeased" or "Your father wishes this done," etc.

We may here endeavour to account for the comparative scantiness of the references to our Blessed Lady in Mark and Matthew, made all the more manifestly scanty by the very full references in Luke. This phenomenon is usually, and we believe quite rightly, accounted for by the death of our Blessed Lady, which may have taken place before the publication in Rome of St. Luke's Gospel.

We have already seen how the Gospel of St. Mark, which is an authentic record of the teaching of St. Peter, has no explicit mention of the Virgin Birth, or indeed of the unique dignity of the Virgin Mother. We have said that one main reason, perhaps the one main reason, of this silence is St. Peter's desire to teach only what he witnessed. Yet another reason may here be mentioned. To stress the Virgin Birth, and especially to stress it in public sermons in Rome itself, could hardly be prudent during the lifetime of our Lady. Rome's intelligence department, which was so accurate and minute in its information as to know the genealogy of a poor Galilean carpenter, might be expected to use its methods of inquiry on the alleged Virgin Mother of the outcast Founder of the Christians.

But Rome could not be kept for ever in ignorance of the Virgin Mother. Indeed there was a certain fitness in the fact that when this woman was beyond the sphere of imperial action the first official declaration of her dignity should be promulgated by St. Luke in Rome itself, and should thereby have the authentication of St. Paul and of St. Peter.

(d) St. Luke's account of the Birth and Infancy of Jesus, for which we must be indebted in great part to the Mother of Jesus, is in no way calculated to revise, but rather to supplement, the account given by St. Matthew. His first two chapters bear everywhere the print of being an official statement made by an eye-witness in order to complete and set in order the great happenings and doings of the beginnings.

A certain quality which we can call only humility runs through these chapters. Thrice does this Virgin Mother of Jesus speak of the "parents" of Jesus—once she publicly in the Temple calls St. Joseph His father. Although a simple statement made to supplement what had been recorded in St. Matthew's Gospel would necessarily bring out her unique dignity, yet her self-witness is never self-assertiveness. She thus took after her Son, who left His sacred dignity of Godhead to be gradually discovered beneath His almost bashful self-witness.

This quality of humility is nowhere seen in greater perfection than in the opening vision to the priest Zachary, husband of our Blessed Lady's cousin. If we had only St. Matthew's account of the beginnings of the Incarnation, we should conclude that Jehovah's first message of the approach of Messianic redemption was to the little home from which the Messias was to spring. But it seems fitting to the handmaiden humility of the Mother of the Messias to record how the first message came to a member of Israel's sacred order of the priesthood, in Israel's most sacred building, the Temple, and in the most sacred hour of official prayer before the very Holy of Holies.

Yet even the self-witness of humility could not hide the dignity of her who called herself "handmaid" when God was calling her to be the human mother of His divine Son. Nothing in the Old Testament was more sacred than was Zachary—an official priest offering sacrifice in the

Temple's Holy place. Yet the dignity of this priest of the Old Testament yields to the dignity of a maiden in her cottage in a hamlet in the Galilean hills.

The contrasts between the angel Gabriel's appearance to the priest in the Temple and to the highland maiden in her home may be best seen in a scheme:

ZACHARY	MARY
LUKE 1:8. When he (Zachary) executed the priestly function.	LUKE 1:26. The angel Gabriel was sent from God into a city of Galilee, called Nazareth.
LUKE 1:9. To offer incense, going into the temple of the Lord...	LUKE 1:27. To a virgin espoused... and the virgin's name was Mary.
LUKE 1:11. There appeared to him an angel...	LUKE 1:28. And the angel being come in said unto her: Hail, full of grace, the Lord is with thee...
LUKE 1:12. And Zachary seeing him was troubled, and fear fell upon him.	LUKE 1:29. Who having heard, was troubled at his saying and thought with herself what manner of salutation this should be.
LUKE 1:13. But the angel said to him: Fear not, Zachary, for thy prayer is heard; and thy wife Elizabeth shall bear thee a son, and thou shalt call his name John...	LUKE 1:30. And the angel said to her: Fear not, Mary, for thou hast found grace with God.
	LUKE 1:31. Behold thou shalt conceive in thy womb and shalt bring forth a son; and thou shalt call his name Jesus.

LUKE 1:32. He shall be great and shall be called the Son of the Most High (the Son of God—v. 35)...

LUKE 1:15. He shall be filled with the Holy Ghost even from his mother's womb....

(LUKE 1:35. The Holy Ghost shall come upon thee....)

LUKE 1:18. And Zachary said to the angel: Whereby shall I know this? for I am an old man and my wife is advanced in years.

LUKE 1:34. And Mary said to the angel: How shall this be done, because I know not man?

LUKE 1:19. And the angel answering said to him: I am Gabriel, who stand before God; and am sent to speak to thee...

LUKE 1:35. And the angel answering said to her: The Holy Ghost shall come upon thee....

LUKE 1:20. And behold, thou shalt be dumb...because thou hast not believed my words.

LUKE 1:38. And Mary said: Behold the handmaid of the Lord. Be it done to me according to thy word. And the angel departed from her.

(i) The term *virgin* is most significantly used by St. Luke. St. Matthew always calls our Blessed Lady the *wife*. "Fear not to take unto thee Mary thy wife"; "and Joseph...took unto him his wife" (Matt. 1:20, 24).

(ii) The parallelism is between a vision given to a priest in the Temple, in the Holy Place, at the solemn hour of sacrifice, and a vision granted to a poor betrothed maiden in a little highland hamlet. The parallelism everywhere confirms the dignity of the Maiden!

(iii) There is a marked contrast between Luke 2:11, "there appeared to him an angel," and Luke 1:26, "the Angel Gabriel *was sent* from God... to a virgin espoused." Not since the time of Eve had such an embassy been sent to a woman. No parallel with this angel-embassy to Mary can be found in the history of the Jewish people.

(iv) Although both messages—to Zachary and to Mary—regard the birth of a child, one embassy is to the husband, the other to the espoused virgin.

(v) "Hail, full of grace, the Lord is with thee" (Luke 1:28). This is the salutation of an ambassador to one of royal rank. An Angel salutes his Queen.

There is no salutation of the priest in the Temple.

(vi) "And Zachary, seeing him, was troubled" (Luke 1:12), because the priest of God was not accustomed to see angels...

"[Mary] having heard, was troubled..." (Luke 1:29).

> Others say that as the Blessed Virgin was accustomed to angelic visions she was not troubled at seeing this angel, but with wonder at hearing what the angel said to her, for she did not think so highly of herself. Wherefore the evangelist does not say that she was troubled at seeing the angel but at his saying. (St. Thomas, *ST* III, q. 30, a. 3, ad 3)

The vision to the Blessed Virgin, as recorded by St. Luke, is also contrasted with the vision to St. Joseph recorded by St. Matthew. St. Thomas notes accurately: "The imagination is indeed a higher power than the exterior senses; but because the senses are the principle of human knowledge the greatest certainty is in them, for the principles of knowledge must needs always be most certain. Consequently Joseph, to whom the angel appeared in sleep, did not have so excellent a vision as the Blessed Virgin" (ibid., ad 2).

(vii) "And thought with herself what manner of salutation this should be" (Luke 1:29). This is in marked contrast with Zachary's fear. The Virgin, accustomed to visions, but disturbed, as the humble of heart are disturbed, by hearing herself praised, is not disturbed in her powers of reasoning. The evangelist represents her as reasoning not about the substance of the vision but about its mode and outcome. Students of mystical phenomena will recognise how much higher is this vision than that granted to Zachary.

(viii) "Fear not, Zachary, for thy prayer is heard" (Luke 1:13).

"Fear not, Mary, for thou hast found grace with God" (Luke 1:30).

How subtle is the contrast! Something that Zachary asked is promised. Something that Mary in her humility could not think to ask is given. An answered prayer is contrasted with an outpoured grace.

(ix) "Thou shalt call his name Jesus" (Luke 1:31). Not only the child is given, but the child's name. Indeed, whereas the Son of Zachary and Elizabeth has but one name, the Son of Mary has three names!

Moreover, this Virgin Mother is of such supreme dignity, that it is she, the woman, and not Joseph, the man, who gives the name.

Note the three names in series of dignity: JESUS; THE SON OF THE MOST HIGH; THE SON OF GOD (Luke 1:31, 32, 35).

(x) "He shall be filled with the Holy Ghost" (Luke 1:15).

"The Holy Ghost shall come upon thee and the power of the most High shall overshadow thee. And therefore also the Holy which shall be born of thee shall be called the SON OF GOD" (Luke 1:35).

The Holy Ghost will come down not on Zachary or Elizabeth but on their son.—The Holy Ghost will come down, with the power of the most High, on Mary, so that the Son of Mary shall be called the SON OF GOD.

(xi) "Whereby shall I know this?" (Luke 1:18).

"How shall this be done?" (Luke 1:34).

Mary's doubt is not a lack of faith, as was Zachary's doubt. It is a mere lack of information.

(xii) "Behold thou shalt be dumb because thou hast not believed my words" (Luke 1:20).

"And Mary said: Behold the handmaid of the Lord. Be it done [FIAT] to me according to thy word. And the angel departed from her" (Luke 1:38).

Here again the contrast between the priest and the Maiden is most striking. The key to this contrast has been expressed by St. Thomas: "It was reasonable that it should be announced to the Blessed Virgin that she was to conceive Christ…in order to show that there is a certain spiritual wedlock between the Son of God and human nature. Wherefore in the Annunciation the Virgin's consent was besought in lieu of that of the whole of human nature" (ibid., a. 1). The Virgin had therefore an official function; and this official function is no less than to represent the whole human race in the wedding with the Son of God.

F. J. SHEED

OF A MOTHER ONLY

The human nature of Christ was not simply a human body animated by a human soul, thus possessing all that the definition of a man requires, suddenly appearing among us. He actually belongs to us. His soul was a direct and individual creation of the Blessed Trinity, just like your soul and my soul; but by His body He was conceived of a human mother, just as you and I.

Of a human mother, notice, but not of a human father. In the sense in which other human beings have a mother and father, He had a mother only. The bodies of other human beings result from the action of an element supplied by their father upon an element supplied by their mother. In the case of Our Lord the effect upon the female element normally produced by the male element was produced simply by a creative act of the will of God. Thus He is a member of Adam's race on His mother's side; He is a Jew on His mother's side; but not upon His father's side, for in the order of human generation He had no father. He was descended from Adam as we all are, but not as much as we all are. None of us derived our souls from Adam, but we all derived our bodies from Adam; whereas He derived His body from Adam only as to part. It follows that

47

we are all related to Him through her, and only through her: we are all His maternal relations, His mother's people.

ॐ ॐ

CAROL

I sing of a maiden
    That is matchless;
King of all kings
    To her son she chose.

He came all so still
    There his mother was,
As dew in April
    That falleth on the grass.

He came all so still
    To his mother's bower,
As dew in April
    That falleth on the flower.

He came all so still
    There his mother lay,
As dew in April
    That falleth on the spray.

THE BOOK OF THE BLESSED VIRGIN

Mother and maiden
  Was never none but she;
Well may such a lady
  Goddes mother be.

HENRI GODIN

WOMAN GOD'S BEST GIFT TO MAN

"A greater gift I could not give man.

And when I sent my Son on earth, he was not hard to please.

No, he was not hard to please—either about food, or lodging, or state in life, or about anything, except his Mother. But about her he was exacting.

He wanted his mother to be a masterpiece, surpassing even my angels, who are already very great masterpieces.

Yes, for her he was exacting—for the woman who was to bring him into the world and awaken his soul and form his heart.

And men are like him. Choosing a woman is always the great affair of their life.

Which doesn't surprise me,"

Says God.

GIOVANNI BOCCACCIO

SONNET

Nor hair of flowing gold, nor eyes alight,
Nor queenly courtesy nor loveliness,
Nor singing throat, nor girlhood tenderness,
Nor countenance angelically bright,
Could enchant down from His sovereign height
The King of Heaven through this world's wickedness,
To be manned in you: Mary all Matchless,
Mother of Mercy, Mirror of Delight;
But your humility could so prevail
To shatter utterly the old disdain
Between God and us; and Heaven's door unbar.
Then, Mary Mother, let it now avail
That we may ascend where blessed you reign,
Following you, to where the faithful are.

MAURICE ZUNDEL

ᘓ ᘓ

THE AGONY OF ST. JOSEPH

The Gospel begins with a tragedy of love, St. Matthew gives us a glimpse into its depths:

> Now the generation of Christ was in this wise.
>
> When as his mother Mary was espoused to Joseph, before they came together she was found with child, of the Holy Ghost. Whereupon Joseph her husband, being a just man, and not willing publicly to expose her, was minded to put her away privately.
>
> But while he thought on these things, behold the Angel of the Lord appeared to him in his sleep saying: Joseph, son of David, fear not to take unto thee Mary thy wife. For that which is conceived in her is of the Holy Ghost.
>
> And she shall bring forth a son, and thou shalt call his name Jesus. For he shall save his people from their sins....
>
> And Joseph rising up from sleep, did as the Angel of the Lord had commanded him, and took unto him his wife. (Matt. 1:18–24)

THERE is not a word too many or too few. In one movement we are brought to the heart of the Mystery; just so it had suddenly confronted Joseph. But we know what the issue was, and Joseph at that time did not.

He loved Mary. From the first moment of their first meeting he had felt that she was unique and that God was entrusting her to him. Was he now called upon to sacrifice her as Abraham had had to steel himself to the immolation of Isaac?

The wound in his heart was immeasurable. The plain fact was there. No denial, no tenderness could alter it. Her very innocence made his anguish more poignant. Another must be guilty, who should take the responsibility for what he had done.

Joseph could not speak of it to her since she had chosen to be silent. Any word would have been an outrage. Silence, his silence, should give him back his liberty for it attested his utter confidence in her.

Thus he came to his decision. And he slept the sleep that relaxes the body but not the soul's pain.

Only if we could concentrate in one heart all the admiration, devotion, fervour that Christian souls were to feel through all generations towards Mary could we form any idea of the love she must have inspired in Joseph, could we divine the immensity of the drama being acted in that hour.

What Dante sang of Beatrice, Joseph could have said in the richest fullness of meaning:

> *He sees perfectly all salvation*
> *Who sees my Lady among women.*

More than any other he felt that human nature was ennobled by her. If he had dared to enter into the espousal, it was to guard the treasure—the treasure which now seemed irremediably lost.

The thought that by this marriage, which their first glance had ratified as an exchange of virginities, he had not been able to prevent a violation that was also a sacrilege, pierced his heart like a sword and sleep could not quiet the pain.

MEANWHILE Mary watched in prayer, suffering in his suffering, living all the agony that her sealed lips could not abate in him.

The yes that bound her soul to Joseph's was all the more irrevocable in that it engaged her fidelity to God, who was the strong foundation of their union.

She had realised that a man of that quality would associate himself with the strange vow that consecrated her to God, would stand between her and the importunity of relations and the demands of custom.

Now that God had willed this miraculous blossoming of her maternity, so that she could not remain alone without raising a host of infamous rumours, was he to be taken from her?

As a virgin, she had consented to marriage; must she renounce marriage as a mother?

It was not, we may imagine, the disgrace she feared, but the wounds that insolence can deal to silence and the brutal invasion of her soul's deepest secrets.

She did not ask to know what the issue should be of a situation into which supreme obedience alone had brought her. She asked only that he should be spared.

I⊤ was then that the Angel intervened:

Joseph—he touches him lightly as a sleeping child—*Son of David*—heir of the promise which shall be fulfilled in you—*fear not to take Mary*—whose name breathes the freshness and the joy of all the dawns—*thy wife*—the title which has made her for ever yours in the sight of God—*for that which is conceived in her*—thus the jubilation of all the Christmas days to come resounds first in you—*is of the Holy Spirit*—who is the eternity of love in the eternity of being.

And he took her to him.

I⊤ is impossible to conceive a more radical opposition to the spirit of possession which transforms so many passions into enslavements, when two beings fall under the intoxication of the absolute empire each exercises over the other, when each sees the other as the one thing necessary—thus promoting each other to the rank of God, and each savouring the adoration which attests his glory as last end. In truth the illusion of adoration which conceals a monstrous egocentrism, which only clutches the more avidly for talking the language of giving, and which finds in the enchantment of the senses the magic source of its ardour—until the day comes when the eyes are opened to see what is really there, no God but a poor shrunken human being, seen in harsh reality for what it is, incapable of stimulating or satisfying.

It happens not infrequently that, in the resentment at having been duped, the emotion that thought it was love turns to a hatred which proves that the original impulse towards the other was only the swollen projection of an ego, quickened by the sap of altruism, but egoism still.

It would, of course, be cruelly unjust were we to fail to see how much of sincerity and nobility and beauty there can be is the complexity of a profound passion in which, even if egocentrism is dominant, there still abides some element of altruists to reflect the divine poverty of love. But it would be no less unjust were we to fail to see the cosmic fatality with which passion often blazes up under the impulsion of the élan vital by which the species seeks to ensure its survival, or the torment brought to many by this insurgence of an instinct which submerges reason and all nobility without bringing them the least ray of light upon its nature, its origin and its end.

Is there, indeed, a more convincing sign of a primordial fall of man than this disastrous deviation in man of an instinct which is fundamentally nothing but the marvellous call of lifer. That this instinct can so often break out in absolute unawareness of its fundamental reason, or what is worse, in the deliberate exclusion of the new life to whose production it ordered; that the ecstasy which should be a creative ecstasy, the magnificent orchestration of an utter giving, the jubilation of two altruisms reaching out to the new being which is the fruit of their love, should be reduced to the mysterious[1] turbulence of a lightless union of two bodies tormented that they must remain two, since there is no communion of souls; surely all this is the most tragic evidence of a life grown exterior to itself, an activity no longer rooted in reality.

---

1. The whole problem here is to place the mystery. We feel that there is a mystery and that it is infinite. But what is it? It is only if we play with the surface of it that we lose our balance and are in peril of being destroyed by it. By going direct to the heart of it, ceasing to remain exterior to it, we come to see its true face and impure phantoms are dispersed. We can but deplore the lack of honesty generally displayed in the training of the creative faculties—indeed the systematic deformation to which they are subjected—in that all the attention of the young is centered upon possible sins, and they are not shown the call to holiness contained in this incredible power which God's trust has confided to them—the power to co-operate with him in the coming into existence of immortal souls, a power which makes the human body the tabernacle of life.

What a curious being is man, ceaselessly troubled by the thirst for the divine, and trying to appease his torment by divinising his body and making an absolute of a physical thrill—until the day when, in the silence of his listening soul, he meets the subsistent altruism of love itself, in which being and giving are one.

Then in truth he realises the essential limitations of possession, the folly of seeking to enclose within the limits of his ego a being not to be satisfied save by the light from heaven.

"So act," says Kant, "as to treat all humanity, whether in your own person or in others, as an end and never as a means." This must be understood of an immediate ordination of the soul to God, of such sort that it cannot attain its own fulfilment unless it loses itself in the abysses of eternal charity and participates in the infinite impulse of the divine altruism.

CLEARLY then a man and a woman—alike called to this divine fulfilment—can give themselves irrevocably to each other only in God and for God: becoming for each other as it were sacraments[2] of the Infinite, sacraments of the love which must units them ever more perfectly to God, in an ever more rigorous yielding up of their own selves:

> Husbands, love your wives, as Christ also loved the church and delivered himself up for it: that he might sanctify it, cleansing it by the laver of water in the word of life. That he might present it to himself a glorious church, not having spot

---

2. I here give the word "sacrament" the analogical meaning of a sensible reality which represents and in some manner communicates the Divine.

or wrinkle, or any such thing, but that it should be holy and without blemish. (Eph. 5:25–27)

And:

Let women be subject to their husbands, as to the Lord: because the husband is the head of the wife: as Christ is the head of the Church. He is the saviour of the [mystical] body. (Eph. 5:23)

If marriage is called to this height, if it is *in Christ* the sacrament which represents and in a certain manner accomplishes the mystery of the church, it is no matter for surprise that the union of two Christians should be in the full stream of the supernatural life, under the primacy of divine Charity, whose ineffable altruism it symbolises in the flesh and confirms in the spirit.[3]

Clearly we must expect to see marriage, obedient to the movement of grace, tend toward that virginity of heart which flowering a flesh that has become as though interior to spirit—so that one thinks not of the soul as in the body but of the body as in the soul.

In fact, one does see marriages in which husband and wife limit their relations strictly to what life itself requires for its continuation,[4] bending their whole purpose to the propagation of new life, in the sole design of offering to God a new temple for the habitation of His Spirit.

---

3. *Summa Theologica* (*ST*) I-II, q. 34, a. 1; II-II, q. 153, a. 2; Supp., q. 41, a. 4.

4. Not through any contempt of the flesh, but in the luminous consciousness of its fundamental ordination to life—which implies that one loves the body with a very great charity and wills its supreme fulfilment in intimate association with the life of the spirit.

Surely we can hope that an ever wider recourse to the sources of the mystical life will direct Christian feeling ever more closely to the ideal represented at its highest by the marriage of Mary and Joseph: so that, in the light of the Wisdom which reconciles extremes by impressing upon all aspects of being the God-centredness of charity, conjugal love itself will become the guardian of virginity, bringing to life a tenderness wholly of God, in God and for God.

ALREADY for us it is a marvellous illumination to realise that the vision of the sexes consecrates the man and the woman to the child, sealing in their flesh the first elements of its corporeal life, and thus in their very bodies prefiguring the profound altruism that is expressed in father-hood and motherhood. And when the vital impulse threatens to darken reason, it is a marvellous refuge to purify its urge in the consideration of the being to which nature has ordained it. Our deep-lying disturbance is calmed as the mystery that has troubled us takes upon itself the face of a child.

It is the child that is the fundamental reason for the instinct that tears at us, the child with the high dignity of its spiritual soul, with the capacity for God which is in him—as in those who have engendered him—a demand for holiness.

As this image grows in strength, it can and does happen that the flesh is calmed, submits more readily to the ordering of the spirit, and feels a pure joy in being in some manner associated with the ever active fecundity of the spirit, which propagates the divine life in the commu-nion of saints.

Now if this reference to the child that may be born and the thought of the sanctuary of Divinity that his soul may be can work so powerfully upon us, what must have been the power of the feeling wrought in Mary and Joseph by the real presence of the Child who was God?

Mary, gathering in her heart all the expectation of Israel, had yet chosen to remain a virgin that her whole being might be one upward surge of love to God.

If she had consented to the tenderness of Joseph, it was that she had either discovered or originated the same design in him. God was to be the sole interchange of a marriage which should consist solely "in the indivisible union of souls."[5]

When Mary became miraculously the Mother of the Saviour, this undertaking received the most ineffable consecration. Her maternity was the supreme fulfilment of her virginity, the divine flower of her giving, the crowning of that love which from the first moment took her utterly out of her own possession, the lily of poverty.

In taking Mary to his home in fulfilment of the ceremony which rendered their marriage definitive, Joseph participated in the maternity of his spouse in the measure in which he was vowed to her virginity. That is to say that he was entirely consecrated to it and that it accomplished his own fecundity, as it did Mary's, in that marvellous fruit which was the work of the Holy Spirit.

Thus it was that she could later say with the most moving tenderness and the most exquisite humility: "Thy father and I have sought thee sorrowing" (Luke 2:48).

Jesus was truly the issue of their marriage, their virginity was fruitful, their flesh exultant and at peace, in the super-eminent realisation of the life-bearing impulse. And as the bond that united them was the

---

5.   *ST* III, q. 29, a. 2.

divine Person of their Child, their marriage was at once holy and eternal, combining in a unique degree all elements of the perfect union—*fides, proles, sacramentum*, fruitfulness, fidelity, indissolubility.

Nor must we forget that to Mary all these titles belong with incontestable primacy: Joseph's virginity was a reflection of her own, his fatherhood was a consequence of her motherhood, and it was by uniting him for ever to Mary that the presence of Jesus confirmed him in grace and established him in that eminent holiness whose rays are over all the Church.

Yet this primacy of Mary did not reverse the natural order which made Joseph the head of the Holy Family. As Jesus obeyed them both, so Mary was lovingly subject to Joseph with that magnanimous humility which makes obedience love's attention to Love.

As with all the mysteries which involve Mary, her marriage was wholly contained in that "be it done unto me according to thy word," which ruled all the movements of her soul according to the demand of the gift of Wisdom, by which she was wholly yielded up to the eternal Wisdom who was His Father's only Son and hers—like the divine song of her poverty in the infinite transparence of a shadowless love.

Eructavit cor meum verbum bonum.
My heart hath uttered a good word. (Ps. 44:2)

Christian husbands and wives, whose love must at times pass through periods of anguished darkness not unlike the Dark Nights of the mystical union, must not forget that the marriage of the Virgin was begun under the sign of sorrow.

She who was in ineffable fullness Wife and Mother will teach them to seek, in setting God ever more perfectly as the centre of all their aims and affections, the solution of the problems that torment them; and she will teach them that wisdom, which is the fruit of a love totally stripped of self, all poverty of spirit, like that which makes of her the

Sedes Sapientiae et Mater pulchrae Dilectionis.
Seat of Wisdom and Mother of Beautiful Love.

ↄ↑ ↄ↑

TWO LETTERS ABOUT ST. JOSEPH

I.

Dear Friend,

You ask me to talk to you from time to time and tell you what my mind is full of. Well, what fills it at the moment is that great and rather mysterious figure, St. Joseph, whose very name provokes a smile from superior persons. He was at once a workman and a gentleman. He was cheerful and silent, with a big noble nose, muscular arms and hands, with one finger often wrapped in rag, as is the way with those who labour in wood. He was not popular with Nazareth folk—they scarcely are who follow a peculiar calling.

And what more singular for a man than virginity, especially at that period? Why had he taken it on himself? How patient he must have been and strong against boredom, like the sun beginning the same round every morning without weariness.

I see him on an autumn day coming back from Caïffa where he went to fetch timber in a broken-down cart. I see him crossing the Sizon at the spot where the plain of Esdraelon unfolds before you, up to the trans-Jordanian mountains, the territory of six of the tribes. The cart sinks to its axles in the mud.

Then I see him in his workshop on a sunny morning. I hear the saw and the hollow noise of balks of timber, and a child coming to look for him and calling, "Joseph, Joseph" (perhaps that has some bearing one way or another on his departure for Jerusalem). His workshop must have been dear to children, as joiners' workshops always are.

Next I see him coming back from Jerusalem with his Bride so young and gentle (not much more than he beloved by the townfolk). I see them landing at home, and the obliging neighbour who had been getting the household ready; the remarks about it all at the well in the evening.

Joseph is the patron of the hidden life, Scripture does not report a single word of his, it is the silence which is Father to the Word. What contrasts are in him! He is the patron of bachelors and of fathers of family, of laymen and contemplatives, of priests and of businessmen! For Joseph was a carpenter. He had to argue with customers and sign small contracts; to follow up bad debts, to plead, to compromise, to buy his goods cheapest while ruminating on the second-hand, and so on.

How his last days of failing health must have been touching between Jesus and Mary, when he could no longer work! I see the coachman of one of those fine ladies who went to the waters at Tiberias drawing up at the sick carpenter's to get the carriage mended. Jesus Himself takes it over and takes the tools from his hands.

All this goes on without a word when the Roman Empire was at its zenith, full of pride and crime like our present civilisation. It is neither Caesar nor Plato. Here are only three poor folk loving one another, and they are going to change the face of the world. It all goes on at the foot of a round mountain called Tabor; and in the distance is seen the long summit of Carmel. The villages near by are called Cana, Nahum, Endor, Mageddo. In three hours you get that brilliant country round the Lake of Genezareth which was then what Aix-les-Bains is today, but now lonely and unpeopled![1]

PRAGUE, 1922

II.

Dear Friend,

I want to unfold a few new ideas on St. Joseph, as your friendly questioning revealed their presence the other day in a dim corner of my mind, where they have ever since been queerly slumbering. But to develop the idea logically, to bring the conclusion pleasantly out of the premiss like the joints of a telescope, is something I do not feel up to every day. My own mind is so geared that at times it works by sudden leaps and bounds. The reader has to get on friendly terms with the stray rabbit that knocks up against the furniture, to watch the right moment to catch him by the paw or by the ears before restoring him to the conjuror's hat! Or if you prefer it, when I clap my hands, I know not what half-dressed actors will answer my summons all together, to take their places in the impromptu

---

1. As to what was made in the workshops of Nazareth, Father Schwelm has given some likely details: "Orders may be pictured in accordance with the known business of the Joiner-Carpenter among the Jews; beams to be squared for the support of the terraces which crowned the houses; harness-shafts and goads for the tillers; beds, trunks, kneading-troughs for housewives, deed-boxes for scribes, merchants, rabbis. Such as a matter of fact are the various works which the Mishna reveals to us as carried on by carpenters" (*Science Sociale* [1909], p. 30).

play of which I am the dishevelled producer. Sooner than construct a scenario, I would rather introduce your own self into the midst of my company and leave you the bother of getting what you can out of it.

The first image that comes into my mind is that Archaic Greek Warrior's Head which I found in a New York auctioneers catalogue. What is gripping about it is its intensely individual character, the terrifying sign of personality in the face, and at the same time its superhuman aspect; a face at once concrete and geometrical, the meeting in a single line-theorem of the daintiest reciprocal propositions of Euclid and Pythagoras; a face both impassioned and hard-bitten. The relation, for instance, between the nose, which is the appraising-point of mastery in the middle of the face, and the two superciliary arcs chiselled like brackets in Algebra, is a thing of endless interest, almost of awe. You might say that the human material has been completely fined down and is wholly subordinated to the mind and the will. The face is the expression, the operation, the direct work of the mind, instead of being its cross-grained and venturesome translation.

The second picture is of quite a different character. A little vignette of the East on the edge of the desert; you see a group consisting of a man, a boy, an ass and a camel. The man is about to tether these animals to the trunk of a dried-up palm-tree, before going on his way with his son into the heart of the wilderness. Even now you anticipate my interpretation by suggesting how the ass of course signifies the imagination, and the camel the memory. For at the point we have got to, these two modest beasts of burden have outworn their usefulness. The ass a bag of trumpets whose monstrous organ is like the very voice of passion and despair, an ass living only on dried hay and hollow straw, with his vast ears and their million hairs as alive as those of Midas to every atmospheric change and every quiver of inspiration. The ass, fit mount for prophets, false ones as well as true, is the very imagination itself, a faculty with big velvet eyes. And as for the camel with its double sack on his back, and his complicated apparatus of cisterns and stomachs, what need have we henceforward of this four-footed alembic? And if I were in the place of the child himself, the dubious Isaac whom we have inwardly begotten to the likeness of our own contemplation, I should not feel entirely secure. What is the use in going to the desert and reaching the inner and inmost wilderness, as Exodus says, if it is merely to bring ourselves with us? What company more odious? Are we not sure to find in there at our service that goat entangled in the briars by the horns—a sacrifice from us to the Eternal?

Again the warrior's head from Magna Graecia has appeared upon the screen. But what takes my attention this time is the helmet on his head. Why do we always represent St. Joseph as a weather-beaten hall-porter whose soft-headed baldness cries out less for the halo than for the smoking-cap? And why should the halo itself always be in the shape of a luminous pancake? Why should not Christians come and call up in many ways the soldier of Christ and fit him out with the helmet proper to his calling? And why should I not draw you myself around my thought of St. Joseph that sort of steely sheath, that unyielding coif, surmounted by a triumphant volute partaking of that mathematic indestructibility of which his features just now took on the comport in our eyes? Then at once this consideration arises in our mind: St. Joseph was above all *the keeper of the Law.* It was in the shelter of the latter that the possibilities of the interior life unfolded in him.

"I am not come to destroy but to fulfil," says our Lord. Now which of us can boast of *fulfilling* perfectly the Commandments with the same

faith and the same attention that he would show to the doctor's *orders*
for instance? To lay down exactly for them the bounds which they have
the right to exact, not just refraining from the contrary of what they require, but positively making them the motive, inwardly assimilated, of
our outward behaviour. Thus it is that our Lord teaches us that the com-
mandment: "Thou shalt not commit adultery," forbids not only adultery
and fornication, but every kind of bad thought. And what keeps out the
bad thought if not the good? Who brings to our business as Christians
that purity, that scrupulousness, that interest, that intensity and that
simplicity in execution, that sort of clinging and pressing towards it of
the heart and the mind effectively fulfilling and giving it meaning, form,
efficacy, and virtue? Who can boast that he has raised obedience to the
level of prescription and that he has properly coloured that dry plan of
which the outline has been entrusted to us of those minute and detailed
specifications of Exodus and Leviticus, the number of steps that can be
made on the Sabbath, as later on the laws of the Church on fasting, on
marriage, on the prohibition of butter during Lent, or of eating fish at
the same time as meat (the Ember days always falling at the most awkward time)—all that made up a sort of artistic restriction on our liberty,
a musical canvas, a tiny but delicate appeal to our attention and our force
of character, an invitation to prefer the law of God to that of the flesh, a
hair between Him and us as fine as the spirit, "One jot," says the Gospel,
"one tittle": Not only the jot which is the simplest of all letters, without
any recoil upon itself, the finger pointing towards heaven, but the dot
which is exactly superposed, that little star above the magnetised nee-
dle. And yet all those easy and wholesome Commandments which God
has given us, not for His sake but for ours, those Commandments of
which we are told that we are to fulfil them to overflowing—what a sorry

mess we made of them before the Holy Father with heartbroken indulgence reduced them to the minimum so as to spare us the transgression! With what ill-humour, what ill-grace, what slowness, what despairing eye on the way out, do we lend ourselves to those which have been left! How differently we should behave if these prescriptions instead of being those of a most wise and kindly God, came from the masseur or the soothsayer? Far from their facility being an aid to their fulfilment, it rendered them contemptible in our eyes. But Joseph who is *par excellence* he that keeps, he that watches and preserves, he who in a good and faithful heart has received all the grain of the Sower without losing one particle, Joseph who is the *Just* man *par excellence*, keeps on repeating to himself the admonitions: "Swift as needles of fire" of the great Psalm 118: "Thy words have I hidden in my heart... Blessed art thou, O Lord: teach me thy justifications.... I will meditate on thy commandments: and I will consider thy ways... For thy testimonies are my meditation... My soul hath coveted too long for thy justifications, at all times.... Give me understanding, and I will search thy law.... Thy judgments are delightful. Thy justifications were the subject of my song in the place of my pilgrimage.... It is good for me that thou hast humbled me, that I may learn thy justifications.... Mine eyes have failed for thy words: When will thou comfort me? ... All thy statutes are the truth.... Your sweet are thy words to my palate! More than honey to my mouth! ... Pierce thou my flesh[2] with thy fear.... I opened my mouth, and I panted, because I longed for thy commandments... Thou art near, O Lord: and all thy ways are truth.... Seven times a day have I given praise to thee, for the

---

2. The Latin says: "My fleshes"—*carnes meas*—every kind of flesh there is in me—all the ways I have of being fleshly.

judgments of thy justice. Much peace have they that love thy law: and to them is no stumbling-block.... I have kept thy commandments and thy testimonies: because all my ways are in thy sight."

Mandata Tua, and again *Mandata Tua, Lex Tua, Lex Tua, Lex Tua, Judicia Tua.*

So speaks the Patron of a happy death.

WASHINGTON, 1932

SISTER MARIS STELLA

꙳ ꙳

SAINT JOSEPH AND THE WORD

Saint Joseph was the most silent saint of all.

No one has written down one word of his for our edification. Not one small word of his was saved unless it is the Word that was the sum of all his life, the precious Word he saved for everyone that It might speak the cross, and not the knife, long, long after he was dead and gone and gathered to his fathers, and never again could he spirit the Child and the young girl, his mother, out of the dangerous city. From all men of all times he was chosen and no other—not one from among the prophets—but this rarely heard and wordless man, to save God's mighty Word.

CARYLL HOUSELANDER

ぐ ぐ

FIAT

The church keeps the Feast of the Annunciation on the twenty-fifth of March. There is still a touch of austerity upon the earth, there is still a silver emptiness in the skies, but expectation of spring is already stirring the human heart, the bud is beginning to break on the tree, the promise of blossom has quickened the spirit of man.

This is the season when we celebrate the wedding of the Holy Spirit with humanity, the wedding of the Spirit of Wisdom and Love with the dust of the earth.

I think the most moving fact in the whole history of mankind is that wherever the Holy Spirit has desired to renew the face of the earth He has chosen to do so through communion with some humble little human creature.

In the instances we know of, it has not been to great or powerful people that the Spirit has come but to the little or the frightened, and we have seen them made new, and known that the subsequent flowering of their lives was nothing else but Christ given to them by that sweet impact.

It is always a love story, a culmination of love between the Spirit of Light and the Bride of the Spirit.

This is something which can happen to everyone now, but it could not have happened to anyone but for the *fiat* of the peasant girl in Nazareth whom the whole world calls Our Lady.

It is in Our Lady that God fell in love with Humanity.

It is upon her that the Dove descended, and the love of God for Humanity culminated in the conception of Christ in the human race.

When she surrendered herself to God, there was indeed a miraculous New Heaven and New Earth. The Spirit entered the world—light and wisdom and love, patience, fortitude, and joy entered the human heart and mind, and in the sight of God a springtime of loveliness woke in the world.

In the virginal emptiness of the girl, Mary of Nazareth, Christ was conceived; it was the wedding of God to a human child, and the wonder of it filled the earth for all time.

"He hath set His tabernacle in the sun: and He as a bridegroom coming out of His bride chamber. His going out is from the end of heaven: and His circuit even to the end thereof" (Psalm 18—Gradual of the Mass of Ember Saturday in Advent).

Christ's insistence on the power of children is very striking.

Almost more than anything else in the Gospel it proves that in God's eyes *being* something comes before *doing* something.

He sets a little child among his apostles as an example of what He loves. He says that heaven is full of children.

Indeed, the Architect of Love has built the door into heaven so low that no one but a small child can pass through it, unless, to get down to a child's little height, he goes in on his knees.

How consistent it is with the incredible tenderness of God that His Christ, the Immortal Child, should be conceived by the power of the

Spirit in the body of a child. That a child should bear a Child, to redeem the world.

Our Lady was at the most fourteen when the angel came to her; perhaps she was younger.

The whole world trembled on the word of a child, on a child's consent.

To what was she asked to consent?

First of all, to the descent of the Holy Spirit, to surrender her littleness to the Infinite Love, and as a result to become the Mother of Christ.

It was so tremendous, yet so passive.

She was not asked to do anything herself, but to let something be done to her.

She was not asked to renounce anything, but to receive an incredible gift.

She was not asked to lead a special kind of life, to retire to the temple and live as a nun, to cultivate suitable virtues or to claim special privileges.

She was simply to remain in the world, to go forward with her marriage to Joseph, to live the life of an artisan's wife, just what she had planned to do when she had no idea that anything out of the ordinary would ever happen to her.

It almost seemed as if God's becoming man and being born of a woman *were* ordinary.

The whole thing was to happen secretly. There was to be no announcement.

The psalmists had hymned Christ's coming on harps of gold. The prophets had foretold it with burning tongues. But now the loudest telling of His presence on earth was to be the heartbeat within the heartbeat of a child.

It was to be a secret and God was so jealous of His secret that He even guarded it at the cost of His little bride's seeming dishonor.

He allowed Joseph to misjudge her, at least for a time.

This proved that God knew Our Lady's trust in Him was absolutely without limit. Everything that He did to her in the future emphasized the same thing. His trust in her trust in Him.

The one thing that He did ask of her was the gift of her humanity. She was to give Him her body and soul unconditionally, and—what in this new light would have seemed absurdly trivial to anyone but the Child Bride of Wisdom—she was to give Him her daily life.

And outwardly it would not differ from the life she would have led if she had not been chosen to be the Bride of the Spirit and the Mother of God at all!

She was not even asked to live it alone with this God who was her own Being and whose Being was to be hers.

No, He asked for her ordinary life shared with Joseph. She was not to neglect her simply human tenderness, her love for any earthly man, because God was her unborn child.

On the contrary, the hands and feet, the heart, the waking, sleeping, and eating that were forming Christ were to form Him in service to Joseph.

Yes, it certainly seemed that God wanted to give the world the impression that it is ordinary for Him to be born of a human creature.

Well, that is a fact. God did mean it to be the ordinary thing, for it is His will that Christ shall be born in every human being's life and not, as a rule, through extraordinary things, but through the ordinary daily life and the human love that people give to one another.

Our Lady said yes.

She said yes for us all.

It was as if the human race were a little dark house, without light or air, locked and latched.

The wind of the Spirit had beaten on the door, rattled the windows, tapped on the dark glass with the tiny hands of flowers, flung golden seed against it, even, in hours of storm, lashed it with the boughs of a great tree—the prophecy of the Cross—and yet the Spirit was outside. But one day, a girl opened the door, and the little house was swept pure and sweet by the wind. Seas of light swept through it, and the light remained in it; and in that little house a Child was born and the Child was God.

Our Lady said yes for the human race. Each one of us must echo that yes for our own lives.

We are all asked if we will surrender what we are, our humanity, our flesh and blood, to the Holy Spirit and allow Christ to fill the emptiness formed by the particular shape of our life.

The surrender that is asked of us includes complete and absolute trust; it must be like Our Lady's surrender, without condition and without reservation.

We shall not be asked to do more than the Mother of God; we shall not be asked to become extraordinary or set apart or to make a hard and fast rule of life or to compile a manual of mortifications or heroic resolutions; we shall not be asked to cultivate our souls like rare hothouse flowers; we shall not, most of us, even be allowed to do that.

What we shall be asked to give is our flesh and blood, our daily life—our thoughts, our service to one another, our affections and loves, our words, our intellect, our waking, working, and sleeping, our ordinary human joys and sorrows—to God.

To surrender all that we are, as we are, to the Spirit of Love in order that our lives may bear Christ into the world—that is what we shall be asked.

Our Lady has made this possible. Her *fiat* was for herself and for us, but if we want God's will to be completed in us as it is in her, we must echo her *fiat*.

This is not quite such an easy thing to do as it seems.

Most people, unless the invitation comes to them in early childhood, have already thrust down fierce roots into the heavy clay of the world. Their hands are already gripping hard on to self-interest. They are already partly paralyzed by fear.

To put aside suddenly every motive except this single one, the forming of Christ in our life, is not so easy for ordinary people who are to remain ordinary.

The surrender we shall make will ask two hard things of us straight away.

The first of these hard things is that through being wed to the Spirit, we shall receive the gift of understanding.

In the world in which we live today, the great understanding given by the Spirit of Wisdom must involve us in a lot of suffering. We shall be obliged to see the wound that sin has inflicted on the people of the world. We shall have X-ray minds; we shall see through the bandages people have laid over the wounds that sin has dealt them; we shall see the Christ in others, and that vision will impose an obligation on us for as long as we live, the obligation of love; when we fail in it, we shall not be able to escape in excuses and distractions as we have done in the past; the failure will afflict us bitterly and always.

We shall have, by virtue of this same gift of understanding, far truer values; and we shall be haunted by a nostalgia for divine things, by a homesickness for God which is not eased in this world even by the presence of God.

And in proportion to our understanding we are likely to be misunderstood; the world does not accept Christ's values. The Beatitudes are madness to the world. "Blessed are the poor, the mourners, the reviled, the persecuted, the calumniated; blessed are those who hunger and thirst after Justice."

People who will not compromise with Christ's values are uncomfortable neighbors for mediocrity; they are likely to be misunderstood; they are often hated.

The world has set up a new set of Beatitudes. They run something like this: "Blessed are the comfortably well off, the cheerful, the highly respected. Blessed are the flattered. Blessed are those who are bored for a good salary on six days in the week and can overeat on the seventh. Blessed are those who are satisfied by social welfare plans and are always willing to compromise; blessed are they when all men respect their rights as citizens and forget that they are men, for their reward will not be very great but they will never be unduly disturbed and they will never disturb the complacency of others."

But if the misunderstanding of the world outside our homes can afflict us, it is nothing at all compared with the misunderstanding of those who are very dear to us (and this is so frequent that it is almost inevitable)—those whom we must love as Mary loved Joseph, that Christ may be formed in us from our very love for them. It is very often those people who are the most bewildered by the mystery of our surrender to the Holy Spirit.

Moreover, just as it was with Our Lady and St. Joseph, the tragedy of misunderstanding between us and our loved ones seems the more baffling because we both are convinced that out own point of view is right, our own actions the fulfilling of God's will.

The words, the actions that hurt us most, often torment those who utter them, just as Joseph must have torn and rent his own mind and heart when he questioned if it were God's will that he should put his young love from him.

Even when this is not so, it is still so natural that it is almost inevitable that those with whom our lives are interlocked should be hurt and frightened when our surrender first takes place, for it will almost certainly reverse all our values and theirs.

One newly converted to the Faith, or reawakened to its meaning, is one who has fallen in love with God, and everyone in the house will feel the presence, the danger of the Divine Lover, whose demands may be uncompromising, may turn the complacency of the middle way topsy-turvy; the presence of the Lover who, to the beloved newly aware of Him, will be utterly irresistible.

He is the Pied Piper to the human heart. He makes people become little children and suddenly tum the world they live in upside down, because they have been enchanted by Him.

Christ the invisible Piper in the home is just like the Catholic Church in the world; other religious, social, political organizations may arouse opposition, but the incurable disquiet of those who fear the Catholic Church is due to the fact that while all the others are systems, the Church is a Person, an incalculable Person, a Person with infinite power and a Child's values: the Person of Jesus Christ.

We know perfectly well that there are often scandals in the Church, that despite her pure heart, her children sometimes grow worldly and base and dress her up with tawdry golden garments which they have woven with black and cunning fingers; sometimes we see nothing but ugliness in her. Yet, even so, she is the refuge and hope of all sinners, the joy and hope of all saints, the life and hope of every living creature; and this is because under this aspect the Church is still Christ, Christ in His Passion, Christ crowned with thorns, His face covered in blood and dirt and the dust of the road that we flung Him down onto. He still remains the one ultimately irresistible Person. This is why the Church is sometimes hated—"Wonder not if the world hate you"—sometimes feared; it is the mystery of utter love which is recognized, if not by the head, at least by the heart, and which no wounding and no disfiguring can hide. "He has no comeliness whereby we shall know Him." But we know Him without comeliness.

St. Peter walked on the stormy sea, but when his faith wavered he began to sink; and Christ rebuked him: "O thou of little faith, why didst thou doubt?"

What courage it would take to try to walk on the sea, even if we could see the face of Christ; but it needs much more courage to leave our false securities, our leaking boats of materialism, and to walk towards Him on the churned-up, angry sea of our civilization.

It would be a heroic thing to do even if we could see Him, but when the face of Christ is hidden in the darkness of our heart, then it requires all the heroism of Our Lady's *fiat*.

No wonder that those whose lives are locked into our own, to whom our well-being is their well-being, are instinctively afraid of this *fiat*, which is so complete a disarming to God.

So completely have we depended upon material things, on money in particular, so terribly are we influenced by fear, that simply to abandon ourselves to God and really to mean it seems to be madness. Those who care for us see that we are in danger of becoming poor, as we really replace the old maxims such as: "Charity begins at home"; "It is my duty to look after myself"; "Business is business," and so on, by, "If a man asks for your coat, give him your cloak also"; "He who saves his life shall lose it; and "Go sell what thou hast and give it to the poor."

"Be it done unto me according to thy word" seems a very bold prayer indeed in view of the words we know God has uttered. It would be easier to sacrifice some big thing to God, to impose some hard rule upon ourselves, than to say, "Do what you like with me."

For us poor creatures it is easier to trust someone who shares our insufficiency than to trust God, whose values are still past our comprehension. Those who love us see our new trust in God, but see with our own old blindness and mistrust. If God does not make us poor and disreputable and unworldly, He is (they think) at least certain to make us ridiculous.

The story of Joseph's bewilderment when he realized that his future wife was going to have a baby is well known and it is well known, too, that Our Lady did not explain.

Her example here teaches us wisdom, when misunderstandings arise because of Christ conceived in us. There is little gained by trying to explain. At that time, the Advent time, His voice is silent in us; it is simply our own heartbeat. Love is more effective then than words.

The only thing to do is to go on loving, to be patient, to suffer the misunderstanding. Explanations even of what *can* be explained seldom heal—and there is so much that cannot be explained.

Even the presence of Christ in us does not do away with our own clumsiness, blindness, stupidity; indeed, sometimes because of *our* limitations, His light is a blinding light to us and we become, for a time, more dense than before. We shall still be irritable, still make mistakes, and still very likely be unaware of how exasperating we are.

Explanations, words, at this stage, may only wound, but love will be a bridge over which at last, in God's time, we shall cross to a better understanding.

It will have to be the love of humility, that is, love informed by humility—long-suffering, patient, and humorous. If we realize that we are a little absurd, such love will come more easily. We must try to be like Our Lady, to make as little fuss as she did about being the Mother of Christ.

CYNEWULF

ℭ ℭ

A MAIDEN RING-ADORNED[†]

Lo, thou the glory of the great earth,
purest of women over all the world
of all who have been since time began,
how right it is that all voices,
all heroes on earth, hail thee, and say
with blithe mood that thou art the bride
of the Noblest One, the sky's King.
So too the highest in the heavens,
Christ's thanes, cry out and sing
that thou art Lady by thy holy might
of the glorious armies, of the race of men
living under the heavens, and of all hell-dwellers.
For thou alone of all mankind
thought gloriously in thy strong mind
that thou wouldst bring to thy Maker thy maidenhood,
give it, sinless. Not again

[†]   Translated by Margaret Williams in her *Wordhoard*.

will such another
a maiden ring-adorned
heaven-homeward
her bright treasure.
bade His high messenger
from His strong glory,
that His Might should speed thee,
the Lord's Son,
in mercy to men,
for ever and ever

come of men
who will thus send
with ever pure heart
So the Lord of triumphs
fly hither
and say to thee
and thou shouldst bear
coming soon
and thou, Maria,
be held unstained.

DIETRICH VON HILDEBRAND

ↂ ↂ

OF CONSECRATED VIRGINITY

Consecrated virginity is, in the first place, freely chosen. A merely external virginity, which has not been deliberately adopted, or even is felt as an unwelcome and painful trial, has as little to do with consecrated virginity as outward poverty forcibly imposed has to do with poverty freely chosen. No doubt a person who is a virgin against his or her will can also be pure, but that purity has no advantage whatsoever over wedded purity, for it brings with it no new value.

On the contrary, the attitude of such a person to sex continues the same as that of a virgin, male or female, before marriage, until all intention of marriage is finally renounced. But this renunciation does not in itself imply a positive choice of virginity, i.e., a determination to belong to God in a special fashion. Even when the circumstances of her life have brought a woman to the conclusion that she is called by God to celibacy and this conviction leads her to renounce matrimony, this is not necessarily an explicit choice of virginity in the positive sense. The renunciation, indeed, alters her attitude to sex as compared with that of a virgin before marriage, inasmuch as it signifies its interior exclusion. It is, however, not a solemn profession of virginity, but a simple acceptance of it, as a man might accept poverty he had not freely chosen, but which God had imposed upon him. Even though—as would be the case if the renunciation were felt as painful—the resignation to God's will possesses a special value, that value in no way differs from that involved in every submissive acceptance of a cross which God lays upon us. In such a case, therefore, no new and distinctive value attaches to the fact of virginity as compared with wedded purity; there is simply the value which submission to God's will, here as in all other circumstances, brings with it. The same value, for example, is present when an unhappy marriage is borne submissively as the dispensation of God's Providence.

Or, again, we may consider a different case. Virginity is here regarded by the subject as her normal condition, because she has no thought of marriage. In this case, no doubt, the virginity is in a certain sense deliberately chosen, as it was not in the previous instance; but with consecrated virginity it has nothing whatever to do. There can be no question of a special value attaching to such virginity. Whether it is deliberately adopted or practised as the obvious course—in any case it is not chosen for the sake of its sublimity and profound significance. It is simply the effect of a purely natural inclination, and as such represents an absence of value as compared with marriage. It is the mere consequence of a defect, inasmuch as the subject is, at least so far as she is personally concerned, incapable of the high value which marriage represents. No greater good occupies her heart in its place: there is nothing but a personal insusceptibility. No doubt such a person may be pure, in which case all the loveliness of purity ennobles her being, but the purity is based, not upon the virginity, but on a general attitude which can equally exist in the married. It is therefore evident that the mere fact of physical virginity as such confers no sort of advantage over marriage, but rather involves a certain lack of value. But even when virginity is freely chosen for the sake of some noble object it is still divided by an entire world from consecrated virginity. If, for example, a woman renounces marriage in order to remain with her parents or chooses a profession whose external conditions exclude marriage, as that of a school teacher—in many countries—virginity is indeed freely chosen, but since its distinctive and profound religious significance is not among the factors which determine the choice it does not necessarily effect a close relation to God. Nor is it even sufficient that virginity be freely chosen because for one reason or another it is believed to be the will of God that the subject should remain in that state, as a man might be convinced that it was God's will that he should adopt some particular secular profession. If, for example, I become convinced that my parents' illness and need of help is a message from God, bidding me renounce marriage, that does not make my virginity in any way consecrated to Him.

The virginity must be directly chosen for God's sake, and for no other reason; and, moreover, in order thereby to belong to Him in a special fashion. It is not sufficient that it be chosen as *willed by God*; it must be referred to Him far more directly; it must be actually *consecrated to God*. It is so consecrated when, in accordance with the words of Our Lord and Saviour Jesus Christ, it is freely chosen "for the kingdom of heaven's sake" (*propter regnum caelorum*). Jesus said to his disciples: "All cannot receive this saying, but they alone to whom it is given. For there are eunuchs which were so born from their mother's womb; and there are eunuchs which were made eunuchs by men; and there are eunuchs which made themselves eunuchs for the kingdom of heaven's sake. Whosoever is able to receive it, let him receive it" (Matt. 19:11–12). The words which state the motive for which consecrated virginity is to be chosen, *"propter regnum caelorum,"* have been differently explained. They are frequently understood of the heavenly reward which awaits the continent. But on this interpretation that which confers upon virginity a peculiar character and a unique value is simply passed over. And, which is the most weighty consideration, this interpretation leaves the specially close relationship to Jesus which this virginity constitutes wholly unexplained. Nor yet, if the words are to be taken as a statement of the motive for which consecrated virginity is chosen, am I able to accept Fr. Wintersig's interpretation, that by *"regnum caelorum"* we are to understand the Church. Our Lord's words are clearly intended to state, not the objective *raison d'etre* of virginity, the reason why there should be virgins, but the *motive* for which the state of virginity should be chosen. The expression "kingdom of heaven" possesses so general and inclusive a meaning in the Gospels, in which "for the kingdom of heaven's sake" so often means the same as "for God's sake," or "for His glory," that it may also be understood as a general statement of the only motive which suits the context. We may again recall the words ascribed to St. Agnes: "The kingdom of this world and every ornament thereof have I scorned for the love of Jesus Christ my Lord, whom I have seen and have loved, in whom I have believed, who is my love's choice." Only when virginity is chosen for the love of Jesus, to belong to Him in particular and closer fashion, and thus to give a special glory to God, does it possess the character which makes it consecrated virginity. Only the will of the individual, who out of love will give herself more closely to Christ, is able—so far as the motive is concerned—to transmute a merely physical into a consecrated virginity. A purely external consecration to God made by the Church over the head of the individual—a contradiction in terms, since it is incompatible with the nature of the Church—could never constitute consecrated Christian virginity.

This can be seen most clearly by comparing with the Christian virgin the consecrated heathen virgin, the Vestal. Not only does the virginity of the Vestal lack the lifelong obligation, whereas Christian virginity, as we shall see later, must of its very nature be *perpetual*, but, what is most important, the virgin's free choice is wanting. The Vestal Virgins were selected and appointed without their consent being asked. And this of itself excludes the motive for which Christian virginity is freely chosen, the love of God, which alone can bring it into a real relation with Him. The heathen virgin was treated as a mere thing and handed over to the god or goddess as a piece of property. This fact altered the entire complexion of this pseudo-religious virginity. Virginity is here regarded from a purely natural standpoint and represents something purely vital. It does not transcend the domain of physical sex. Whereas Christian virginity with its supernatural radiance destroys every hankering after the charm of sex, with this natural virginity this is by no means the case. On the contrary it is, so to speak, from the sexual point of view that this virginity is valued. We need only contemplate the impassable gulf which divides the natural vital ideal of virginity as exemplified in Artemis from the hallowed chastity of the most blessed and ever Virgin Mary.

The most radical distinction, however, between heathen and Christian virginity, that which determines this absolute difference of quality between them, does not consist simply in the fact that the former lacks the free choice indispensable for a genuine self-dedication to God and the love which is its motive, but primarily in this: the deity to whom the pagan virgin was consecrated was a false god, not the true God, One in Three, who reveals Himself to us in Jesus. Moreover, heathen virginity does not owe its form to the operation of the supernatural union of human nature with God effected by the Incarnation of the eternal Word and the consequent nuptial relationship of the Church and Jesus. But it remains true that the *kind* of consecration also determines the difference of quality between the two. The love of God, here the indispensable motive, which is essentially grounded in God's infinite love for man, whom He so loved that He gave His only begotten Son, and which is actually a participation of this divine Love, is thinkable only within the mystical body of Christ.

Consecrated virginity, therefore, can exist only when a member of Christ's mystical body freely chooses perpetual virginity, out of love for Him, and, moreover, in order by that virginity to belong more closely to Him. But even this is not enough. Yet another factor is essential—the explicit vow of virginity. It is by the social act of vowing that the virgin first places her virginity in the hands of God and solemnly binds herself to it.

The distinctive nature of consecrated virginity as compared with every other is now clear. Only when the virginity is freely chosen out of love to Jesus in order to belong more closely to Him and to give glory to God, and, moreover, vowed in perpetuity, does it become consecrated virginity.

VINCENT MCNABB, O.P.

ↄℓ ↄℓ

THE VISITATION

And Mary rising up in those days, went into the hill country with haste into a city of Juda.

And she entered into the house of Zachary and saluted Elizabeth.

And it came to pass that when Elizabeth heard the salutation of Mary, the infant leaped in her womb. And Elizabeth was filled with the Holy Ghost.

And she cried out with a loud voice and said: Blessed art thou among women and blessed is the fruit of thy womb.

And whence is this to me that the mother of my Lord should come to me?

For behold as soon as the voice of thy salutation sounded in my ears, the infant in my womb leaped for joy.

And blessed art thou that hast believed, because those things shall be accomplished that were spoken to thee by the Lord.

And Mary said: My soul doth magnify the Lord.

And my spirit hath rejoiced in God my Saviour.

Because he hath regarded the humility of his handmaid: for behold from henceforth all generations shall call me blessed.

Because he that is mighty hath done great things to me: and holy is his name.

And his mercy is from generation unto generations, to them that fear him.

He hath shewed might in his arm: he hath scattered the proud in the conceit of their heart.

He hath put down the mighty from their seat and hath exalted the humble.

He hath filled the hungry with good things: and the rich he hath sent empty away.

He hath received Israel his servant, being mindful of his mercy.

As he spoke to our fathers: to Abraham and to his seed for ever.

And Mary abode with her about three months. And she returned to her own house. (Luke 1:39–56)

IN ORDER to weigh accurately St. Luke's witness to the dignity of the Blessed Virgin in his account of the Visitation, we must bear in mind the Hebrew character of St. Luke's Gospel. Lagrange says that St. Luke's Gospel contains more Hebrew forms than do Matthew and Mark, indeed many more than Mark. Biblical critics who see these facts do not always see the significance of the facts. In the present matter it is most significant that there is a much less decided Hebrew character in St. Mark's (i.e., St. Peter's) Gospel, published in Rome, than in St. Luke's (i.e., St. Paul's) Gospel, also published later on in Rome. The contrast between the Petrine gospel and the Pauline gospel is almost paradoxical. In his Epistle to the Galatians St. Paul had written "to me was committed the gospel of the uncircumcision as to Peter was that of the circumcision" (Gal. 2:7). Yet the gospels which were due to their teaching are so different from what might seem the plain meaning of these words to the Galatians, that we might take St. Paul to be the Apostle of the Jews and St. Peter the Doctor of the Gentiles.

To the present writer this seems a fact of first magnitude for understanding the meaning of St. Paul's, and indeed of St. Peter's, epistles, as well as St. Luke's Gospel and Acts. In the hastily written letter to the Galatians St. Paul had so identified himself with the Gentiles and had so accentuated the imperfections of the Jewish dispensation that he had spoken of the *Curse of the Law* (Gal. 3:13).

A cursory examination of St. Paul's subsequent epistles will make it clear that he was at pains later on to explain this phrase, one of the "things hard to be understood" which are to be found, as St. Peter so meekly says, in St. Paul's epistles. Gradually his explanation became fuller and fuller until it reached the fulness of the immortal letter to the Hebrews. Midway between the epistle to the Gentile Galatians and the Hebrews stands St. Luke's work in the Gospel and the Acts.

The Gospel of St. Luke is Hebrew not only in phrase but in aim. It is in many ways the glorification of the Jews, and especially of the Jewish priesthood. Its Jewish and priestly character is paralleled only by the Epistle to the Hebrews; for which, indeed, it seems to prepare the way.

(i) It alone shows that the first message about the Incarnation was to a priest—in Jerusalem—in the Temple—at the hour of sacrifice. The Temple is here a House of Prayer and not a Den of Thieves.

(ii) Luke suggests that even our Blessed Lady, the only human parent of the Son of God, was of the priestly tribe, being a kinswoman of Elizabeth who "was of the daughters of Aaron."

(iii) Luke alone tells us that St. John the Baptist was of the priestly tribe.

(iv) Had St. Luke not written his Gospel the Church of today would not know that it was in the Temple that our Blessed Lord received his first public recognition. Moreover, this presentation was in fulfilment of that law which St. Pau had spoken of as the Curse of the Law: "they carried him to Jerusalem...as it is written in *The Law of the Lord*" (Luke 2:22–23).

(v) Luke tells us that even the legal rite of circumcision, so great a matter of discussion by the Pauline group, was faithfully observed by our Blessed Saviour.

(vi) It tells us, moreover, that year by year the Holy Family left their home in Galilee to go up to Jerusalem for the Passover (Luke 2:41).

This is an astounding narrative from the pen of the Greek physician; and still more from the Gentile follower of the Doctor of the Gentiles.

But whatever else is doubtful in the Gospel of St. Luke, it is certain that this Gospel, published in Rome by the faithful secretary of St. Paul, is unsaying the phrase *Curse of the Law* by everywhere glorifying the Jewish people and especially the Jewish law with its sacrifice and sacrificing priesthood.

All this serves to bring out the dignity of the Virgin Mother whom St. Luke describes as visiting the home (in Jerusalem?) of the priest to whom had been sent the first official news of the Incarnation (Luke 1).

15. He shall be filled with the Holy Ghost even from his mother's womb.

41. When Elizabeth heard the salutation of Mary the infant leaped in her womb. And Elizabeth was filled with the Holy Ghost.

42. And she cried out with a loud voice and said: BLESSED ART THOU

AMONG WOMEN, AND BLESSED IS
THE FRUIT OF THY WOMB.

15. He shall be great before the Lord.

43. And whence is this to me that the MOTHER OF MY LORD should come to me?

14. And thou shall have joy and gladness.

44. For behold as soon as the voice of thy salutation sounded in my ears, the infant in my womb leaped for joy.

20. Thou shalt be dumb and shalt not be able to speak...because thou hast not believed my words, which shall be fulfilled in their time.

45. And blessed art thou that hast believed, because those things shall be accomplished that were spoken to thee by the Lord.

(i) As Zachary, the priest, is still dumb, speech must be left to Elizabeth. Later on, when the punishment of dumbness has been finished, Zachary will be seen to have seconded in thought what Elizabeth had said in welcoming "the Mother of her Lord."

(ii) The special outpouring of the Holy Ghost, foretold by the angel at his visit to Zachary, awaits the visit of our Blessed Lady. But this fulness is greater than the words of the angel would have led us to expect. Not only the child but the mother is filled with the Holy Ghost.

(iii) "Blessed art thou among women," etc. To feel the force of this inspired cry of Elizabeth we must remember that of all the daughters of Sion none had received such a gift as Elizabeth had received by the miraculous begetting of St. John the Baptist. Yet this does not conceal from her the greater gift to her young kinswoman, Mary. Only virgin begetting could be greater than miraculous begetting.

(iv) "The mother of my Lord." This is a clear enunciation of the fact that the Son of Mary was the Messias, whom her son was to "go before in the spirit and power of Elias."

(v) Luke 1:14. "Thou shalt have joy and gladness; and many shall rejoice in his nativity."

Luke 1:44. "For behold as soon as the voice of thy salutation sounded in my ears, the infant in my womb leaped for joy."

Again it is through the coming of Mary (bearing her Son) that the prophecy of joy is fulfilled. Mary is graciously called, in her Litany, "Cause of Our Joy"; even though another of her titles is "Mother of Sorrows."

(vi) The unbelief of the priest, Zachary (Luke 1:20), is contrasted with the belief of the Virgin Mother. Indeed Zachary's unbelief is punished by his own dumbness; whilst Mary's belief is rewarded by the inspiration and sanctification of Elizabeth and her unborn child.

(vii) Two phrases are contrasted, "the words that shall be fulfilled in their time" and "those things shall be accomplished which were spoken to thee by the Lord." Literally "there shall be a consummation of the things spoken to her by the Lord." The word "consummation" is only twice used in the New Testament: here and in the Epistle to the Hebrews (7:11); "If then perfection was by the Levitical priesthood... what further need was there that another priest should arise according to the order of Melchisedech, and not be called according to the order of Aaron?" Strangely enough it is a daughter of Aaron who, speaks to the Mother of the Priest of the order of Melchisedech, and foretells that through her faith the perfection or consummation would come.

And Zachary his father was filled with the Holy Ghost. And
he *prophesied* saying: Blessed be the Lord God of Israel:
because he hath visited and wrought the redemption of his
people.

And hath raised up an horn of salvation to us, in the house of
   David his servant.

As he spoke by the mouth of his holy prophets, who are from
   the beginning.

Salvation from our enemies and from the hand of all that hate
   us.

To perform mercy to our fathers and to remember his holy
   testament.

The oath, which he swore to Abraham our father, that he
   would grant to us, that being delivered from the hand of our
   enemies, we may serve him without fear:

In holiness and justice before him, all our days.

And thou, child, shalt be called the prophet of the Highest:
   for thou shalt go before the face of the Lord to prepare his
   ways: To give knowledge of salvation to his people, unto
   the remission of their sins.

Through the bowels of the mercy of our God, in which the
   Orient from on high hath visited us:

To enlighten them that sit in darkness and in the shadow
   of death: to direct our feet into the way of peace. (Luke
   1:67–79)

(i) The word *prophesied* is remarkable. In the gospels there is only
one other mention of any individual prophesying. St. John says: "And

this he spoke not of himself; but, being the high priest of that year, he *prophesied* that Jesus should die for the nation" (John 11:51). It is significant that there are, thus, in the gospels but two mentions of actual prophesying: the priest Zachary, and the high priest Caiphas.

(ii) This prophetical witness of Zachary's Canticle to Mary's dignity may be summed up in the words of Lagrange:

> If Mary was present and if her presence has inspired Zachary, as Origen thinks (Hom. 10), Luke may have been alluding to the situation and to the birth of St. John. But Luke has hinted that Mary was no longer present.... The canticle is, then, the reply of Zachary to the question raised about John, and this reply *comprises all that the presence of Mary had revealed to the two spouses.* The Canticle consists of seven distichs. Everyone recognizes a pause after v. 76. The first four distichs take up the theme of the *Magnificat,* while leaving out what is proper to Mary.

What greater witness could there be to the dignity of this Virgin Mother of Christ, than that a priest in the solemn words of inspired prophecy should be re-echoing her inspired words?

GERARD MANLEY HOPKINS

THE MAY MAGNIFICAT

May is Mary's month, and I
Muse at that and wonder why:
   Her Feasts follow reason.
   Dated due to season—

Candlemas, Lady Day;
But the Lady Month, May,
   Why fasten that upon her,
   With a feasting in her honour?

Is it only its being brighter
Than the most are must delight her?
   Is it opportunest
   And flowers finds soonest?

Ask of her, the mighty mother:
Her reply puts this other
   Question: What is Spring?—
   Growth in every thing—

Flesh and fleece, fur and feather,
Grass and greenworld all together;
Star-eyed strawberry-breasted
Throstle above her nested

Cluster of bugle blue eggs thin
Forms and warms the life within;
And bird and blossom swell
In sod or sheath or shell.

All things rising, all things sizing
Mary sees, sympathising
With that world of good.
Nature's motherhood.

Their magnifying of each its kind
With delight calls to mind
How she did in her stored
Magnify the Lord.

Well but there was more than this:
Spring's universal bliss
Much, had much to say
To offering Mary May.

When drop-of-blood-and-foam-dapple
Bloom lights the orchard-apple

And thicket and thorp are merry
With silver-surfèd cherry.

And azuring-over greybell makes
Wood banks and brakes wash wet like lakes
    And magic cuckoocall
    Caps, clears, and clinches all—

This ecstasy all through mothering earth
Tells Mary her mirth till Christ's birth
    To remember and exultation
    In God who was her salvation.

CARYLL HOUSELANDER

☙ ☙

ADVENT

Advent is the season of the seed: Christ loved this symbol of the seed.

The seed, He said, is the Word of God sown in the human heart.

"The Kingdom of Heaven is like to a grain of mustard seed."

"So is the Kingdom of God as if a man should cast seed into the earth."

Even his own life-blood: "Unless the seed falling into the earth die, how shall the earth be sown?"

The Advent, the seed of the world's life, was hidden in Our Lady.

The Advent, the seed in the earth, the seed of the Bread of Life was in her.

Like the golden harvest in the darkness of the earth, the Glory of God was shrined in her darkness.

Advent is the season of the secret, the secret of the growth of Christ, of Divine Love growing in silence.

It is the season of humility, silence, and growth.

For nine months Christ grew in His Mother's body. By His own will she fanned Him from herself, from the simplicity of her daily life.

She had nothing to give Him but herself.

He asked for nothing else.

Working, eating, sleeping, she was forming His body from hers. His flesh and blood. From her humanity she gave Him His humanity.

Walking in the streets of Nazareth to do her shopping, to visit her friends, she set His feet on the path of Jerusalem.

Washing, weaving, kneading, sweeping, her hands prepared His hands for the nails.

Every beat of her heart gave Him His heart to love with, His heart to be broken by love.

All her experience of the world about her was gathered to Christ growing in her.

Looking upon the flowers, she gave Him human sight. Talking with her neighbors she gave Him a human voice. The voice we still hear in the silence of souls saying: "Consider the lilies of the field."

Sleeping in her still room she gave Him the sleep of the child in the cradle, the sleep of the young man rocked in the storm-tossed boat.

Breaking and eating the bread, drinking the wine of the country, she gave Him His flesh and blood; she prepared the Host for the Mass.

This time of Advent is absolutely essential to our contemplation too.

If we have truly given our humanity to be changed into Christ, it is essential to us that we do not disturb this time of growth.

It is a time of darkness, of faith. We shall not see Christ's radiance in our lives yet; it is still hidden in our darkness; nevertheless, we must believe that He is growing in our lives; we must believe it so firmly that we cannot help relating everything, literally everything, to this almost incredible reality.

This attitude it is which makes every moment of every day and night a prayer.

In itself it is a purification, but without the tense resolution and anxiety of self-conscious aim.

How could it be possible that anyone who was conscious that Christ desired to see the world with his eyes would look willingly on anything evil? Or knowing that He wished to work with his hands, do any work that was shoddy, any work that was not as near perfection as human nature can achieve?

Who, knowing that his ears must listen for Christ, could listen to blasphemy or to the dreary dirtiness of so much of our conversation, or could fail to listen to the voice of a world like ours with compassion?

Above all, who, knowing that Christ asked for his heart to love with, for his heart to bear the burden of the love of God, could fail to discover that in every pulsation of his own life there is prayer?

This Advent awareness does not lead to a selfish preoccupation with self; it does not exclude outgoing love to others—far from it. It leads to them inevitably, but it prevents such acts and words of love from becoming distractions. It makes the very doing of them reminders of the Presence of Christ in us.

It is through doing them that we can preserve the secrecy of Advent without failing to offer the loveliness of Christ in us to others.

Everyone knows how terrible it is to come into contact with those people who have an undisciplined missionary urge, who, having received some grace, are continually trying to force the same grace on others, to *compel* them not only to be convened but to be converted in the same way and with precisely the same results as themselves.

Such people seem to wish to dictate to the Holy Ghost. God is to inspire their neighbor to see things just as they do, to join the same societies, to plunge into the same activities. They go about like the scriptural monster, seeking whom they may devour. They insist that their victims have obvious vocations to assist in, or even be completely sacrificed to, their own interests. Very often they unwittingly tear out the tender little shoot of Christ-life that was pushing up against the dark, heavy clay, and when the poor victim has been devoured, he is handed over, spiritless and broken, as a predigested morsel for the next one-hundred-percent zealot who comes along.

Our Lady's example is very different to this.

When a woman is carrying a child, she develops a certain instinct of self-defense. It is not selfishness; it is not egoism. It is an absorption into the life within, a folding of self like a little tent around the child's frailty, a God-like instinct to cherish, and some day to bring forth, the life. A closing upon it like the petals of a flower closing upon the dew that shines in its heart.

This is precisely the attitude we must have to Christ, the Life within us, in the Advent of our contemplation.

We could scrub the floor for a tired friend, or dress a wound for a patient in a hospital, or lay the table and wash up for the family; but we shall not do it in martyr spirit or with that worse spirit of self-congratulation, of feeling that we are making *ourselves* more perfect, more unselfish, more positively kind.

We shall do it just for one thing, that our hands make Christ's hands in our life, that our service may let Christ serve through us, that our patience may bring Christ's patience back to the world.

By His own will Christ was dependent on Mary during Advent: He was absolutely helpless; He could go nowhere but where she chose to take Him; He could not speak; Her breathing was His breath; His heart beat in the beating of her heart.

Today Christ is dependent upon men. In the Host, He is literally put into a man's hands. A man must carry Him to the dying, must take Him into the prisons, workhouses, and hospitals, must carry Him in a tiny pyx over the heart onto the field of battle, must give Him to little children and "lay Him by" in His "leaflight" house of gold.

The modern world's feverish struggle for unbridled, often unlicensed, freedom is answered by the bound, enclosed helplessness and dependence of Christ—Christ in the womb, Christ in the Host, Christ in the tomb.

This dependence of Christ lays a great trust upon us. During this tender time of Advent we must carry Him in our hearts to wherever He wants to go, and there are many places to which He may never go unless we take Him to them.

None of us know when the loveliest hour of our life is striking. It may be when we take Christ for the first time to that grey office in the city where we work, to the wretched lodging of that poor man who is an outcast, to the nursery of that pampered child, to the battleship, airfield, or camp.

Charles de Foucauld, a young French soldier of our own day, became a priest and a hermit in the desert, where he was murdered by some of the Arabs whom he had come to serve. His life as a missionary hermit seemed no more than a quixotic spiritual adventure, a tilting at windmills on the desert sands, but he knew and said that it was worthwhile for just one thing: because he was there, the Sacred Host was there.

It mattered nothing if the heroic priest could not utter the wonder that was in his heart; the Blessed Sacrament was there in the desert; Christ was there, silent, helpless, dependent on a creature; that which His servant could not utter in words, Christ would utter, in His own time, in silence.

Sometimes it may seem to us that there is no purpose in our lives, that going day after day for years to this office or that school or factory is nothing else but waste and weariness. But it may be that God has sent us there because but for us Christ would not be there. If our being there means that Christ is there, that alone makes it worth while.

THERE is one exquisite incident in Our Lady's Advent in which this is clearly seen: the Visitation.

"And Mary rising up in those days went into the hill country with haste, into a city of Juda."

How lyrical that is, the opening sentence of St. Luke's description of the Visitation. We can feel the rush of warmth and kindness, the sudden urgency of love that sent that girl hurrying over the hills. "Those days" in which she rose on that impulse were the days in which Christ was being formed in her, the impulse was His impulse.

Many women, if they were expecting a child, would refuse to hurry over the hills on a visit of pure kindness. They would say they had a duty to themselves and to their unborn child which came before anything or anyone else.

The Mother of God considered no such thing. Elizabeth was going to have a child, too, and although Mary's own child was God, she could not forget Elizabeth's need—almost incredible to us, but characteristic of her.

She greeted her cousin Elizabeth, and at the sound of her voice, John quickened in his mother's womb and leapt for joy.

"I am come," said Christ, "that they may have life, and may have it more abundantly." Even before He was born His presence gave life.

With what piercing shoots of joy does this story of Christ unfold! First the conception of a child in a child's heart, and then this first salutation, an infant leaping for joy in his mother's womb, knowing the hidden Christ and leaping into life.

How did Elizabeth herself know what had happened to Our Lady? What made her realize that this little cousin who was so familiar to her was the mother of her God?

She knew it by the child within herself, by the quickening into life which was a leap of joy.

If we practice this contemplation taught and shown to us by Our Lady, we will find that our experience is like hers.

If Christ is growing in us, if we are at peace, recollected, because we know that however insignificant our life seems to be, from it He is forming Himself; if we go with eager wills, "in haste," to wherever our circumstances compel us, because we believe that He desires to be in that place, we shall find that we are driven more and more to act on the impulse of His love.

And the answer we shall get from others to those impulses will be an awakening into life, or the leap into joy of the already wakened life within them.

It is not necessary at this stage of our contemplation to speak to others of the mystery of life growing in us. It is only necessary to give ourselves to that life, all that we are, to pray without ceasing, not by a continual effort to concentrate our minds but by a growing awareness that Christ is being formed in our lives from what we are. We must trust Him for this, because it is not a time to see His face, we must possess Him secretly and in darkness, as the earth possesses the seed. We must not try to force Christ's growth in us, but with a deep gratitude for the light burning secretly in our darkness, we must fold our concentrated love upon Him like earth, surrounding, holding, and nourishing the seed.

We must be swift to obey the winged impulses of His Love, carrying Him to wherever He longs to be; and those who recognize His presence will be stirred, like Elizabeth, with new life. They will know His presence, not by any special beauty or power shown by us, but in the way that the bud knows the presence of the light, by an unfolding in themselves, a putting forth of their own beauty.

It seems that this is Christ's favorite way of being recognized, that He prefers to be known, not by His own human features, but by the quickening of His own life in the heart, which is the response to His coming.

When John recognized Him, He was hidden in His mother's womb. After the Resurrection He was known, not by His familiar features, but by the love in Magdalene's heart, the fire in the heart of the travellers to Emmaus, and the wound in His own heart handled by Thomas.

ROSA MYSTICA

There is no rose of such virtue
As is the rose that bear Jesu:
　　Alleluia.

For in this rose containéd was
Heaven and earth in little space:
　　Res Miranda.

By that rose we may well see
There be one God in Persons Three:
　　Pares forma.

The angels sang, the shepherds too:
Gloria in Excelsis Deo:
　　Gaudeamus.

Leave we all this worldly mirth
And follow we this joyful birth:
　　Transeamus.

SIGRID UNDSET

CHRISTMAS AND EPIPHANY

From our Lord's Birthday until Epiphany the Church keeps Christmas. The five joyful mysteries of the rosary, the antiphons and the prayers in the offices for Christmas, are the central point of our worship. Near the altar where He Himself lives clothed in the white garb of the Host, and where His mark, the crucifix, is placed over the tabernacle, there is now a crib—a little picture of the stable where the Word who became Flesh first opened His infant eyes. And round the little figure of the Christ Child stands the likeness of the first things and the first people who met His glance when He by whom all things were made came to His own in the form of a servant.

The crib is not meant only to be a picture of a room where a Jewish carpenter and a young woman sought shelter for the night—a night nineteen hundred odd years ago. For so little did the world take account of what came to pass that night so long ago, in the outhouse of the caravanserai at Bethlehem, that no one definitely knows the year in which it happened or at what time of the year; and indeed during the first centuries after Christ's birth opinion is so divided that there is scarcely a month that has not been suggested as the actual Christmas month.

Elegit eam Deus et praelegit eam. "God hath chosen her and forechosen her," it says in the Office. In God is all eternity, and from eternity was Mary destined to bear under her heart Him—

> quem terra, pontus, sidera
> colunt, adorant, praedicant

—"whom earth and sea and sky honour, worship and preach."

> O gloriosa Domina
> excelsa supra sidera
> qui te creavit provide
> lactasti sacro ubere.

—"Oh, glorious lady, exalted over the stars, thou hast tended and nourished from thy holy breast Him who created thee."

THE angels bring tidings of the Child's birth to some shepherds who are out on the hills outside the village: a star rises up and beckons some astrologers from a land far away in the East to set out on a long journey. But the rest of the world—all those Mediterranean countries which Roman law and Roman peace had knit together into a single empire, where the people bowed under the yoke of Rome, proud to be her citizens or embittered by her oppression—the world which some hundreds of years later was to date its history from His birth, slept quietly through the night of this great happening. And St. Luke troubles himself so little with descriptions of places that, except by tradition, we know really nothing about the room where Mary brought forth her Son—only that it was outside the inn and that it was a stable. We hear that the shepherds hurried to Bethlehem to see what it was that the Lord had signified to them. But it does not tell us that they brought any gifts to the little family. When in representations of the crib we make the shepherds bring their presents to the Child Jesus it is perhaps something that we have imagined, for St. Matthew says most particularly that it was the Wise Men from the East who brought gifts. Or perhaps we are thinking of ourselves—that this is what we should have done if we had been the shepherds.

For the crib should also remind us of what Tauler says in his Christmas sermon: "*Unto us a Child is born and unto us a Son is given. He is ours and He is altogether and fully our own: He belongs to us more than does anything else. He is always and unceasingly born in us.*"

Yes, in that way—whispers the chilly, cautious person of the present day—in that way we also can join you in the stable. If the little Boy in the crib is a symbol of the longing in each one of us for something beyond the bounds of sense, of our presentiments of immortality, then we also can remain with the shepherds in the stable. We can worship Mary's child, we moderns, as a symbol or as a type, as the great Teacher, a genius, a superman. But as God in Man? "*Genuisti eum—qui te fecit?*" Mary, could you have brought forth Him who created you? Can you expect us to believe this sort of thing in the twentieth century?

Is it not a truth, which modern children cannot avoid, that human beings are blood-cousins of the apes, and that our earth is only a small-holding in the world of space? Can we be so pretentious as to believe that He by whom all was made should have become our brother in the arms of this poor young girl? How is it possible that the omnipotence which, through an immeasurable span of time, has planted a myriad of suns, should be one with the delicate, tiny infant in the arms of the maid from Nazareth, sheltered by her hair and shawl as they droop from her bending head? We know, of course, that it was anthropomorphism when the old people spoke of the heavens as the work of God's hands and of wisdom issuing from the mouth of the Most High, the firstborn of all created: *"I alone have encompassed the circuit of Heaven and have penetrated into the bottom of the deep, and have walked in the waves of the sea."*

And how is it possible that this omnipotence should be in those gentle hands which the Child holds folded together under His chin, and in the delicate little feet crossed over one another as He stretches them out? On the crown of His head the blood pulses and quivers under the skin with the quick heart-beats of the newly born. And this little quickly working heart, you say, is the glowing seat of love?

BUT is it possible that the anthropomorphism of any other era has been quite so coarse or so vulgar as our own—when we transfer to our vision of God our own stupid wretched respect for anything that is purely colossal in dimension, for records in magnitude and for enormous unwieldy numbers? As our knowledge of nature has widened our picture of the time and space which God encompasses we lose, more and more, our ability to believe that the strength of the Almighty to permeate all things is indeed all-powerful. And involuntarily we picture God as a sort of cosmic landlord: it is impossible for Him to interest Himself in and to love each individual life which crawls on this remote speck of earth amidst the dancing of the myriad stars. Or we look on Him as a sort of Director-General for the great combine of the United Solar Systems. He cannot know personally each little functionary who works on a small planet rotating around a sun of quite insignificant size.

In her book about the Sisters of Tøss, Elsbeth Staglin describes the meditation of Sister Jüzi Schulthasin: "She recognized also that nothing can remain hidden from God, and that the smallest gnat cannot put down its foot without God seeing it. And impossible though it is that a man should poke out another's eye without his victim's knowledge, it would be a thousand times more impossible that God should not know all things."

But this was in other days—the fifteenth century. In those times certainly men thought of God too much in terms of man—we have always realized this. And as long as our souls have to work through physical organs they must involuntarily help themselves by using similitudes taken from the plane of observation open to the senses, so as to clarify the representation. Thus inevitably everything tends to become anthropomorphic in the language of metaphor.

In the museums and monastic libraries of Europe there is volume alter volume of illuminated manuscripts of the Middle Ages. If ever artists have worked to give their best and most beautiful without a thought of winning glory or credit for themselves it is certainly these anonymous painters whose identity is only occasionally discovered, and whose reward went to the whole brotherhood. This is indeed art for art's sake, pure, clean passion for beauty—inspired by the mind's constant occupation with the loveliness of God, who has created us in His image so that we also can realise the joy of creation. Year in and year out the craftsman sat and painted borders with flowers shining like jewels, with playful birds and clinging vines on the smooth, yellowish-white parchment. The frames, which the capital letters required, he filled out with a polished gold ground and with delightful small pictures, the faces of saints, not so big as wood anemones, drawn with lines as fine as the veins in the anemone petals. Not for a moment would the artist contemplate that anyone else except himself should suspect what an amount of care and love he had put into his work, but each little flower was painted in order that it should be perfect in itself, without thought whether anyone was ever going to study it carefully. Perhaps this maker of pictures can help us, not to understand, but to get a glimmering of God's great love for His creation, which caused him to come to His own as a little child in a crib and to die upon the cross to save each soul He had created in His image—to perfect one tiny little forget-me-not in the eternal manuscript of the universe.

> Genuit puerpera Regem, cui nomen aeternum, et
> gaudia matris habens cum virginitatis honore,
> nec primam similem visa est, nec habere sequentem.

—"She was in labour and brought forth the King whose name is eternal; she had the happiness of a mother together with the honour of virginity; she was seen to have no equal either before or since."

But it is exactly this which is contrary to nature—that a woman can be both mother and virgin. (As a matter of fact, it is on this point that our laboratories seem to be threatening our conception of nature with a complete and terrible revolution, for they promise to show us generations of beings whose mothers, although they will not bear the garland of virginity, yet will not know man.) But at the time when Christendom began, all races, both within and without the borders of the Roman Empire, worshipped a deity of motherhood and a mother of gods and supernaturally begotten gods and demi-gods. And the people of the

Middle Ages, as all enlightened people know, fall into two groups: a smaller group of men and women of the Church who did not take much notice of the improbable or unnatural stories which the other group, all the other people, accepted in every detail without thinking.

It is not, however, quite accurate to say that these stories of the birth of gods without an earthly father shadow forth a virgin mother, in the Christian sense. They suppose a god in a human home or in an animal's lair, or they imagine some other material contact—lightning, gold rain falling over the maiden, or she eats a magic fruit or swallows a pine-needle.

But whatever legend or adventure the people of those days believed and related, it leaves no trace in Our Lady's own little book of hours— the layfolk's book of hours which the Middle Ages produced and which we pray every day. Not for a moment have these legends either there or in the priest's breviary been incorporated in the story of Our Lady's mysterious preferment; Mother and Daughter, God's Mother and God's Daughter, she stands alone.

> Genuisti qui te fecit.
> *Thou hast borne Him who created Thee.*

> Sancta et immaculata virginitas, quibus te laudibus efferam nescio; quia quem caeli capere non poterant, tuo gremio contulisti.
> *Holy and Immaculate virginity—I know not with what words of praise I can exalt Thee. For Him whom the Heavens could not contain, thou hast nursed in thy lap.*

O Virgo virginum, quomodo fiet istud? Quia primam simi-
lem visa est nec habere sequentem.
O Virgin of virgins, how shall this be? (For she was seen to have
no equal either before or since.)

Filiae Jerusalem, quid me admiramini? Divinum est myste-
rium hoc, quod cernitis.
Daughters of Jerusalem, why look ye so wonderingly upon me?
The mystery which you see is of the Godhead.

Oh, Mary, lift up the Child. Lift Him up that we may gaze upon Him!

BUT what ground have we for humility if we are blood-relations of
the apes? For in that case it seems we are a particularly gifted branch
with strong powers of development, continuing from the days of the
cave-dwellers and the flint ages to the world-war and after it.

Before the Child in Mary's arms we try to be not proud but humble—to see that we are dust and nothing at all. Whence have we received
our gifts and talents, and what have we done with them? We think of
the ways that these small feet shall tread, of the words that this Child's
mouth shall speak, of all that these eyes have seen and of what they shall
see in our hearts—evil and ugliness and love and laughter; our sickness
and deformities, our leprosy which His hands have taken away; the rec-
ompense with which we recompensed Him, the crown with which we
crowned Him, and how finally we lifted Him up towards the skies—and
how He from the height of the Cross saved His people from their sins.
And when we have discerned all this a little and have promised our Lord
our love and fidelity—what has our love and fidelity been worth!

EPIPHANY—after Epiphany comes Lent, and the Church tries to lead us along the way to Maundy Thursday and Good Friday and Easter.

But up to Epiphany it is Christmas. Jesus is still safe in her arms who has called herself the handmaid of the Lord.

MARY indeed was unstained by inherited sin—but that does not mean that here on earth she was omniscient or could see into the future. I wonder what she thought of the message of the angel to the Child she bore: *"The Lord God shall give unto Him the throne of David His father: and he shall reign in the house of Jacob for ever, and of His kingdom there shall be no end."* When Joseph came and they had to travel to Bethlehem, to David's town, the time was drawing near when the Child was to see the light. We do not know; perhaps Mary had thought that everything would happen very differently—but the Son of the Most High was to be born in an outhouse. She wrapped Him up and laid Him in the manger and watched over His sleep, and when He was awake she warmed Him and fed Him at her breast.

Some shepherds came and wished to see the Child, and they told of visions of angels and angels' words.

And Mary hides all these things in her heart and meditates on them.

FORTY days later she and Joseph take the Child and go up to Jerusalem to fulfil the law of Moses, and to present the firstborn of a young mother to the Lord and buy him free from the temple service.

As they enter the Temple bearing the infant and two young doves, the offering of the poor, they are met by an old man. He comes over to them, this old stranger, and wants to hold the Child that Mary carries. And when Simeon has Jesus in his arms he praises God and breaks into words: "*Now Thou dost dismiss Thy servant, O Lord, according to Thy word, in peace*"—*Nunc Dimittis*, we read in Compline, the evening prayer in the Book of Hours. If we realise the mystery of Christmas well enough, we should say the same for ourselves every evening.

And Simeon blessed Mary and Joseph—a peculiar blessing, for he says that *this Child is set for the fall and for the resurrection of many*, and he speaks of *a sword* which *shall pierce* the heart of the mother, the young heart which hides within itself so many wonderful words and has meditated on so many mysteries.

ぞ ぞ

A BRAVE-HEARTED MAID[†]

Be glad in heart,
for thy comfort,
hold thy hoard locked,
in thine own mind.
True comrades sometimes
word-promises grow faint;
going swiftly in showers.
There is one faith,
one Baptism,
One Lord of peoples
its good things and joys,
through this passing earth,
hidden in gloom,
well screened by trees,
till a brave-hearted maid
There it pleased Him

grow great before the Lord
and build up glory;
bind fast thy thought
Many a thing is unknown.
fall away, tired,
so fares this world,
shaping its destiny.
one living Lord,
one Father everlasting,
who made the world,
Its glory grew
stood for a long time
under a dark helm,
overshadowed by darkness,
grew up among mankind,
who shaped all life,

---

†   Translated by Margaret Williams in her *Wordhoard*.

the Holy Ghost,
bright on her breast
who was the beginning

to dwell in her treasure-house
shone the radiant Child
of all light.

THE HOLLY AND THE IVY

The holly and the ivy,
When they are both full grown.
Of all the trees that are in the wood,
The holly bears the crown:
 The rising of the sun
 And the running of the deer,
 The playing of the merry organ,
 Sweet singing in the choir.

The holly bears a blossom,
As white as the lily flower,
And Mary bore sweet Jesus Christ
To be our Saviour:

The holly bears a berry,
As red as any blood,
And Mary bore sweet Jesus Christ
To do poor sinners good:

The holly bears a prickle,
As sharp as any thorn,
And Mary bore sweet Jesus Christ
On Christmas day in the morn:

The holly bears a bark,
As bitter as any gall,
And Mary bore sweet Jesus Christ
For to redeem us all:

The holly and the ivy,
When they are both full grown,
Of all the trees that are in the wood.
The holly bears the crown:

The rising of the sun
And the running of the deer,
The playing of the merry organ,
Sweet singing in the choir.

ROBERT SOUTHWELL

COME TO YOUR HEAVEN, YOU HEAVENLY CHOIRS

Come to your heaven, you heavenly choirs!
Earth hath the heaven of your desires;
Remove your dwelling to your God,
A stall is now his best abode;
Sith men their homage do deny,
Come, angels, all their fault supply.

His chilling cold doth heat require,
Come, seraphins, in lieu of fire;
This little ark no cover hath,
Let cherubs' wings his body swathe;
Come, Raphael, this Babe must eat,
Provide our little Toby meat.

Let Gabriel be now his groom,
That first took up his earthly room;
Let Michael stand in his defence,
Whom love hath linked to feeble sense;

THE BOOK OF THE BLESSED VIRGIN

Let graces rock when he doth cry,
And angels sing his lullaby.

The same you saw in heavenly seat,
Is he that now sucks Mary's teat;
Agnize[1] your King a mortal wight,
His borrowed weed lets not your sight;
Come, kiss the manger where he lies,
That is your bliss above the skies.

This little Babe, so few days old,
Is come to rifle Satan's fold;
And hell doth at his presence quake,
Though he himself for cold do shake;
For in this week unarmèd wise
The gates of hell he will surprise.

With tears he fights and wins the field,
His naked breast stands for a shield;
His battering shot are babish cries,
His arrows looks of weeping eyes,
His martial ensigns cold and need,
And feeble flesh his warrior's steed.

His camp is pitchèd in a stall,
His bulwark but a broken wall;

---

1.   *Agnize*, know, recognize.

The crib his trench, hay-stalks his stakes,
Of shepherds he his muster makes;
And thus, as sure his foe to wound,
The angels' trumps alarum sound.

My soul, with Christ join thou in fight;
Stick to the tents that he hath pight[2];
Within his crib is surest ward,
This little Babe will be thy guard;
If thou wilt foil thy foes with joy,
Then flit not from this heavenly boy.

2. *Pight*, pitched.

RICHARD CRASHAW

THE NATIVITY

Come we shepherds whose blest sight
Hath met love's noon in Nature's night;
   Come lift we up our loftier song
   And wake the sun that lies too long.

To all our world of well-stol'n joy
   He[1] slept; and dreamt of no such thing.
While we found out Heaven's fairer eye
   And kiss'd the cradle of our King.
Tell him he rises now, too late
   To show us aught worth looking at.

Tell him we now can show him more
   Than he e'er show'd to mortal sight;
Than he himself e'er saw before;
   Which to be seen needs not his light.

---

1.   The Sun.

THE BOOK OF THE BLESSED VIRGIN

Tell him, Tityrus, where th' hast been
Tell him, Thyrsis, what th' hast seen.

TITYRUS. *Gloomy night embrac'd the place*
    Where the noble infant lay.
The babe look'd up and show'd his face;
    In spite of darkness, it was day.
It was thy day, sweet! and did rise
Not from the East, but from thine eyes.

THYRSIS. *Winter chid aloud; and sent*
    The angry North to wage his wars.
The North forgot his fierce intent;
    And left perfumes in stead of scars.
By those sweet eyes' persuasive pow'rs
Where he meant frost, he scatter'd flow'rs.

BOTH. *We saw thee in thy balmy nest,*
    Young dawn of our eternal day!
We saw thine eyes break from their East
    And chase the trembling shades away.
We saw thee; and we blest the sight,
We saw thee by thine own sweet light.

TITYRUS. *Poor world (said I) what wilt thou do*
    To entertain this starry stranger?
Is this the best thou canst bestow?
    A cold, and not too cleanly, manger?

Contend, ye pow'rs of heav'n and earth
To fit a bed for this huge birth.

THYRSIS. *Proud world, said I; cease your contest*
    And let the mighty babe alone.
The Phoenix builds the Phoenix' nest.
    Love's architecture is his own.
The babe whose birth embraves this morn,
Made his own bed e'er he was born.

TITYRUS. *I saw the curl'd drops, soft and slow,*
    Come hovering o'er the place's head;
Off'ring their whitest sheets of snow
    To furnish the fair infant's bed.
Forbear, said I; be not too bold.
Your fleece is white but 'tis too cold.

THYRSIS. *I saw the obsequious Seraphims*
    Their rosy fleece of fire bestow.
For well they now can spare their wings
    Since Heav'n itself lies here below.
Well done, said I: but are you sure
Your down so wann, will pass for pure?

TITYRUS. *No no, your King's not yet to seek*
    Where to repose his royal head;
See see, how soon his new-bloom'd cheek
    Twixt mother's breasts is gone to bed.

Sweet choice, said we! no way but so
Not to lie cold, yet asleep in snow.

BOTH. *We saw thee in thy balmy nest.*
    Bright dawn of our eternal day!
We saw thine eyes break from their East
    And chase the trembling shades away.
We saw thee: and we blest the sight.
We saw thee, by thine own sweet light.

FULL CHORUS.
    Wellcome, all Wonders in one sight!
Eternity shut in a span.
    Summer in Winter.   Day in Night.
Heaven in earth, and God in Man
Great little one! whose all-embracing birth
Lifts earth to heaven, stoops heav'n to earth.

    Wellcome. Though nor to gold nor silk,
To more than Caesar's birth right is;
    Two sister-seas of Virgin-Milk,
With many a rarely-temper'd kiss
That breathes at once both Maid and Mother,
Warms in the one, cools in the other.

    Wellcome, though not to those gay flyes
Gilded ith' Beames of earthly kings;
    Slippery soules in smiling eyes;

But to poor Shepherds, home-spun things:
Whose Wealth's their flock; whose wit to be
Well read in their simplicity.

Yet when young April's husband showers
Shall blesse the fruitfull Maia's bed,
We'll bring the First-born of her flowers
To kisse thy Feet and crown thy Head.
To thee, dread Lamb! whose love must keep
The Shepherds, more than they the sheep.

To Thee, meek Majesty! soft King
Of simple Graces and sweet Loves.
Each of us his lamb will bring
Each his pair of silver Doves;
Till burnt at last in fire of Thy fair eyes,
Our selves become our own best Sacrifice.

EDWARD LEEN, C.S.SP.

THE PRESENTATION IN THE TEMPLE

The first days of our Blessed Saviour on earth must have been ones of ecstatic joy for Mary. During those forty days of seclusion which the law imposed on her she tasted to its fullest measure the happiness of motherhood. She had given birth to a Son, and the Babe she held in her arms was none other than her God and her Creator, whilst He was at the same time flesh of her flesh, and there ran in His veins her own most pure blood. Exempt from all the pain and weakness which is the lot of all other mothers since the sin of Eve, she was, from the very first moment, able to lavish on Jesus all the care and attention that His helplessness— the helplessness of the Omnipotent—needed. Every service that His infant state demanded of her was given with wondrous promptitude and solicitude. To feel God powerless in one's arms and to be able to minister to His wants would be, in itself, sufficient to bewilder any soul less strong and less simple than Mary's. She did not pass her time in motionless adoration. *Her maternal attentions to the needs of her Child were her worship. She never for an instant lost sight of the Babe in her adoration of her God, nor did her deep realisation of the Godhead cause her to forget for a moment the necessities of the Child.* The physical tie which bound her to Jesus, the natural maternal instincts which such a tie created, would make it impossible to lose sight of the fact that the Being that nestled in her arms and looked to her for help, protection and sustenance was her Child. The absolute independence of the God did not dim her perception and full realisation of the complete dependence of the Babe. But this profound sense of the reality of the Infancy of Jesus did not cloud her vision of the power and the glory and the divinity that lay hidden under the frail, fleshly love became mingled and identified with the creature's most perfect love of its Creator. She had not two loves of Jesus in her heart, the love of a mother for her child and the love of a creature for its God. The latter simply passed into the former, undergoing, in the passage, a marked transformation. In the Mother's love for her Child the creature's love of the Creator was touched with a marvellous devotedness, tenderness and reverent familiarity. How grateful she must have been for the law which bade her, though it did not bind her, to wrap herself up in that deep retirement, where she could, without interruption, allow herself to be penetrated through and through with the joy that inundated her soul.

Mary's uninterrupted bliss did not last for long. As is usual in the case of all God's spiritual consolations, her joy was a prelude to a trial which was to plunge her into the deepest grief. The Levitical Law ordained that every mother that had borne a male child should, after forty days of seclusion, redeem her right to take part once more in the service of religion by the offering of sacrifice. The women of Israel were considered to have contracted a legal stain in childbirth, and for this reason were obliged to offer a young pigeon or a dove as a sin offering. By this sacrifice was taken away their legal disability and after the offering of it they were free once more to attend the ceremonies of the divine worship. The sacrifice of atonement was followed by one of worship and thanksgiving. A young lamb, or in the case of the poor, still another dove or pigeon, was offered in holocaust to the Supreme Being. It was a solemn protestation by which the young mother acknowledged God as the Source and Author of her own life, and that other fresh young life that God had made her instrumental in bringing forth. These sacrifices made, the law furthermore enjoined that the child, if it were the first-born, should be consecrated to God. Originally, amongst the theocratic people, the first-born male child was, in virtue of this primogeniture, destined to exercise the sacerdotal functions on behalf of his family. He was consecrated to God from his birth. The establishment of a definite sacerdotal caste by the setting apart of the tribe of Levi for the service of the tabernacle took away the *raison d'etre* of this custom. But still, God, to mark His absolute rights over His people and to engrave deeply on their memories their deliverance from the bondage of Egypt, when all the first-born of men and animals were, on their account, afflicted with death, claimed the eldest male child of each family as His own. That the child might be in a position to be brought back to the bosom of his family there was demanded from the parents a ransom of five shekels. The coming of Jesus signified the passing of the priesthood of Aaron. In the presentation[1] of the Son of Mary there returned the primitive signification of the offering. In what a perfect sense was He, the eldest born of Mary, consecrated to God and the divine service! How absolutely did He belong to God! How perfectly was He priest on behalf of His family—which was the whole human race!

---

1. Fillion notes that the Greek word used by St. Luke and translated by the English term "present" has a religious meaning. It corresponds to a Hebrew word which was used to designate the offering of sacrifices with bloodshedding and those without blood-shedding. It literally means—to bring near to the altar. *Vie de N.S.J.C.*, vol. 1, ch. 3.

Mary had not contracted any stain in bringing forth her Child. The Body of Jesus had been formed outside all the ordinary laws of conception, and in a miraculous manner, by the Holy Ghost. Although really and truly His Mother, she preserved her virginity unimpaired. She was a virgin before, during and after the delivery of Our Lord. She did not, therefore, come under the prescriptions of the Law; yet it never occurred to her to demand exemption from its application in her regard, on the grounds of the privilege that had been bestowed on her by God.

She had conceived solely by the operation of the Holy Ghost, and so preserved the fairness of virginity whilst acquiring the glory of motherhood. Yet, so far was she from wishing to proclaim aloud her great and incomparable dignity, that she chose rather to hide it from the eyes of men by humbly submitting to the law that weighed upon the daughters of Israel. In all the scenes of the sacred infancy transmitted to us by the skilful and artistic pen of St. Luke it is instructive to note the close association between the Mother and the Child. The same characteristic is to be observed in the narrative of St. Matthew. Of the Magi, he says, that "entering the house, they found the child with Mary His Mother." Now the grouping of these two thus constantly, as if they formed a certain unity, is not unintentional. Neither is it due to the physical state of dependence in which the infant actually was with regard to her who had given Him birth. It is literally true that He needed the help of her sustaining arms to be presented to the gaze of His worshippers. But this natural necessity is not the reason for the insistence of the inspired writers in grouping together the mother and the child in all these incidents, when the infant is the centre of admiration, praise and worship. The close association of the two, so strongly stressed, points to a certain inseparability between them in the function which was to be the life-work of the Child. The two were to be as one in realising the purpose of the existence in the flesh of the Son of the Most High. This being so, it is eminently fitting that this intimate outward association should be a visible sign of inward unity of sentiments, tastes and aspirations. The external closeness marks the inner oneness. It is remarkable how naturally, from the moment of the Incarnation, the interior dispositions of Mary harmonise with those of her divine Child. Instinctively His ways become hers. The dispositions of the Mother easily mingle with and melt into those of the Child. What His tastes would inspire in the way cf action becomes her choice. Her ways perfectly reflect His. She instinctively enters into His predilections. Jesus in a spirit of humility and in obedience to the law, from which He was exempt, willed that for Him should be paid the ransom that was customary in the case of every first-born male child in Israel. In a similar spirit of humility and obedience Mary submitted herself to the rule of purification which she had no obligation to undergo. She practises the same self-effacement and observes the same silence as her Child. The words said about Jesus and the actions done concerning Him do not betray her into opening her lips and proclaiming aloud to all the wonders of which she holds the secret. She veils herself in modesty and retirement; she says nothing; she allows the incidents to speak for themselves; she watches and adores the action of Divine Providence in regard to her Child, and is content to store up all these things in her mind, in order to meditate on them at her leisure and to probe ever more deeply into the unfathomable mystery contained in every incident of the human-divine life that is gradually manifesting itself before the eyes of men. So now, too, after the forty days of her seeming purification were accomplished she preserves a complete silence on all that has taken place within her, leaving the revelation of it to the moment determined

147

by God's Providence. Angels, Elizabeth, Shepherds, Kings, Simeon and Anna, all in their turn speak and proclaim aloud the glories of her Divine Son, whose splendour is reflected on her who gave Him birth; *she* is silent and buries herself in profound meditation on all she sees and hears.

Her virginity was very dear to her. So dear was it that she was ready to forego the wonderful privilege of the Divine Maternity rather than surrender it, and yet she is content to have it known only to God and herself, and to pass before men as one who had foregone that virginity for the bonds of marriage and the dignity of motherhood. She maintains the same silence and reserve when she stands before the Jewish priest and allows him to make the legal sin offering on her behalf, although she is absolutely sinless and exempt from all that concupiscence which is the fruit and the punishment of sin. Only God Himself saw the depths of humility in her soul; only the Child she held in her arms could sound the deep abasement involved in the humble acceptance of the conditions of existence that enveloped her as a daughter of a sinful race, even though she herself was sinless.

Who of those that saw her passing that day up the steps of the temple, mounting from the Court of the Women to the entrance into the Court of Israel, could suspect that this modest, unassuming, poorly clad, if dignified Jewish mother was in anything distinguished from those others who on that same occasion were, with her, pressing towards the gate of Nicanor to fulfil the same legal obligation as she. Nothing in her revealed to the careless glance that the humble and unassuming Nazarene, bringing the offering of the two poor turtle doves, was in very truth at that moment the Queen of them all, the Queen of the whole universe, the Sovereign of the invisible world of spirits, the Mother of the great God, who was Ruler and Judge of all in Heaven and on earth and under the earth. That quiet exterior, from which there radiated an indefinable grace and dignity, revealed nothing of all this. And it is ever so. Nearly all that is great and noble, elevated and divine in the world of souls, is as a rule destined to escape the notice and observation of men. It is only the eye of faith, purified by prayer and close union with God, that can pierce the disguise and perceive the divine realities that lie concealed in what seem to be the ordinary things of this world. It is only the practised eye of the saint, trained to observe objects in the immaterial atmosphere of the supernatural world—so disturbing for the ordinary vision of the ordinary unsanctified human being—that can discern Jesus Christ in the poor, in the outcast and in the abandoned; it is only he that is accustomed to close and constant communing with God that can see the action of God's Providence in the vicissitudes of human life, and that can read the wonderful realities of God's grace that are contained in the very least symbols and rites of our holy religion. St. Teresa could say with truth that she felt she could gladly die on behalf, not of the faith, but of the very least rubric prescribed in the ceremonies in which that faith expresses its worship.

What a wonderful contrast Mary, in her reserve, presents to our way of acting! It requires constant effort on our part to keep in check our desires to make parade of every gift or talent that is ours by nature or by grace. Even really spiritual persons are not exempt from some anxiety lest their qualities should remain in obscurity. They fear that they themselves may not be able to turn their qualities to account unless they are credited by men with the possession of these qualities. Mary's example should save us from this foolish and idle fear. If we seek but one thing only, namely, to abide in union with God and seek only His esteem and regard, we can be certain that God will on His side make such use of us and our talents as is most conducive to His glory. We must, like Mary, wait for God's manifestation, and in the meantime carefully guard from the eyes of those around us those gifts, whatever they be, with which we may have been favoured by God.

There is a tradition that there was a remarkable resemblance in feature between Mary and Jesus. However this may be, we can be certain, from the testimony of the Gospels, delivered to us in many a suggestive trait, that there was a wonderful likeness between them in lineaments of soul. Jesus had shown His predilection for poverty by His choice of the place and circumstances of His birth. Mary, who had brought Him to birth in her mind, before bringing Him into the world, was quick to learn, and prompt to put in practice, the lesson conveyed by this choice. Poverty and lowliness are a hard election, a harder election than suffering, because they entail greater disabilities in the eyes of our fellow-men, even in the eyes of the good and high-minded amongst them. Poverty, no matter how one may wish to ignore the fact, does carry a stigma with it, and a certain shame. It should not be so. It is unnatural that it should. But the fact remains. The great bitterness of Poverty lies in this, that it carries with it a certain powerlessness, helplessness and dependence on others. Patronage and not esteem is the lot of the poor. And human nature shrinks from the one as much as it hungers for the other. Poverty takes from man many of the possibilities of achievement—as achievement is understood by mankind. To noble natures it is easy to give and it is distressing to have to receive. The poor have little means of giving, few opportunities of bestowing help or conferring favours. Under the disabilities that attend the absence of this world's goods it is difficult to preserve one's dignity. It is much easier to be dignified in suffering than in poverty. It was these very disabilities that weigh so heavily on the poor that determined the choice of Jesus and, as a consequence, that of Mary. We are not surprised to find her coming to the temple bearing in her hand two doves—the offering of the poor. It is significant that St. Luke is not content with remarking that she offered the usual sacrifice, but that he takes care to note that her offering was that of the very poor. We see, of course, at a distance that poverty did not detract from but rather enhanced the nobility of Jesus and of Mary. But at the time and in the judgment of those around them was it the same? Is it not our own instinct—the instinct, that is, of nature, though not of grace—to be condescending towards the poor and to treat with them as if, in truth, the absence of worldly means did lower a man's dignity and worth? Is it not the instinct of the man who is well-to-do, even though he be fairly religious minded, to regard his less fortunate fellow-man as one who is not quite his equal as far as human values go? It takes all the force of the example of our Heavenly Mother to rectify in us this false view, this false attitude towards life. But with that example before him, who does not feel stirred to love and esteem not only detachment of spirit, but real and actual want, should God send it? The Christian, having before his eyes the vision of God Incarnate and of the creature nearest to Him on earth evincing such a predilection for what St. Francis poetically terms his "Lady Poverty," has no excuse if he continues to give his esteem to wealth as such and to repute the poor, because of their poverty, as of less worth than himself. It is the characteristic of all great souls to rise superior to this ignoble prejudice.

True holiness consists in the sympathetic entering into the views and feelings of Our Blessed Lord. How different Jesus would have been for us had He chosen to come in the guise of wealth rather than in that of poverty! For the vast majority of mankind condemned to a life of lowliness and want, He would have been a God removed from them, not an Emmanuel, a God dwelling with them, and sharing their life and their hard lot. But to the poor, all come with ease and without constraint—rich and poor alike. The poor are eminently accessible, whereas wealth, owing to the inequalities it generates, invariably erects a barrier, even when the rich are not very worldly or overweening. Poverty, it is true, has its rewards. To be sure, it makes us powerless, but in Christ's Kingdom power is made perfect in infirmity. St. Paul could say: "I will glory in nothing but my infirmities" (2 Cor. 12:5).

When Jesus, in the hands of the priest, had renewed interiorly the unreserved offering of Himself to God in sacrifice that He had already made at His entrance into the world and when Mary had, in lowliness, obedience and humility, conformed herself to the requirements of the law, the whole Mystery of the Presentation was not consummated. Before Mary left the temple she was to be called on to make a sacrifice that was to cost her more than did the renouncement, in the estimation of men, of the real dignity and the true wealth that was hers, in virtue of her high prerogatives. In the holocaust of the second dove she gladly prostrated her whole being before God, and offered herself unreservedly to the purposes of the Divine Will.

God took her instantly at her word. *The unalloyed joys of her Motherhood were of short duration.* As she was making her way forth she found herself confronted by an old man of holy and venerable appearance. With a confidence and reverent assurance which she could not resist he took the child from her arms. Gazing on the infant face, and his whole countenance illumined by prophetic fire, gladness and enthusiasm, he cried aloud: "Now Thou dost dismiss Thy servant, O Lord, according to Thy word, in peace. Because my eyes have seen Thy salvation, which

Thou hast prepared before the face of all peoples: a light to the revelation of the Gentiles, and the glory of Thy people Israel." Whilst Mary was contemplating the wondrous vision that was opened up to her mental gaze by this glorious prophecy, the eyes of Simeon were turned from the face of the Child and fell on the Mother. It is hard for us to know how far Mary's vision had, up to this moment, pierced the veil of futurity and seen what lay before her Divine Son. She had read and pondered on the oracles of the prophets relating to the Messias. Many of them spoke of glory, but several also set forth details of suffering and ignominy. God did not reveal all to her from the beginning; she dimly surmised what was to be. She had too much spiritual understanding to be carried away, as her countrymen were, by the predictions concerning the Messias, which seemed to promise a career of earthly triumph and glory. The visions of the prophets that unfolded scenes of bitter suffering and final rejection were for her the ones that more literally than the others set forth the earthly destiny of her child. She had forebodings of what was to come. It is to be remembered that Mary's great dignity did not freeze or etherealise in her the natural instincts of a mother's heart. Hence it was that she would strive to drive her heavy forebodings into the background of her consciousness. Her maternal love would wrestle with her fears and seek to conquer them. She would be moved by her love for her child to believe against her own spiritual convictions. It is a different thing to labour under the foreboding of an impending woe and to be brought face to face with the bitter reality. Whoever has seen on a human countenance the impression of anguish which suffuses it as dire previsions of some great sorrow harden into certainty can realise what Mary underwent as the concluding words of Simeon's prophecy smote her ears. He said: "Behold this Child is set for the fall, and for the resurrection of many in Israel, and for a sign which shall be contradicted. And thy own soul a sword shall pierce, that out of many hearts thoughts may be revealed."

As Simeon's words penetrated to her consciousness, her soul was flooded with light and the shadows that had hitherto clothed the harsh reality disappeared. She at last grasped in all their significance those texts which set forth the history of a Messias destined for pain and death. The Messias is now her Son, and she realises that her own Child is to undergo, at the hands of His own people, contradiction and trial and a rejection culminating in a cruel death. For some only, not for all, was her Son to prove a Saviour: for many, through their own fault, He was to be an occasion of utter and irreparable spiritual disaster. "And Simeon said to Mary, His Mother: Behold this Child is set for the fall, and for the resurrection of many in Israel, and for a sign which shall be contra-dicted." Her mother's heart was wrung with anguish as the sword of this bitter prophecy was plunged into it and as it turned in the deep wound it made. It was the first of those Seven Sorrows by which her soul was cru-cified with a crucifixion that resembled that of her Son. She shuddered when she saw what she should be called on to bear. She knew that it was demanded of her that she should acquiesce in the awful dispensation of Providence that was presented to her in vision. She realised that it would be asked of her not merely to allow the Divine Will to pursue its course or merely submit to that Will in its dealings with Jesus, but also, over and above all that, to identify her will with that Will of God, and to make the voluntary sacrifice of the gift that had been placed in her arms. She was asked to will the sacrifice of Jesus. It was an incredibly hard thing to ask of a mother. It was much to ask her to accept—but to will it! That was something which would be demanded only of a sanctity like Mary's.

And her sanctity did not flinch before God's demand. And when her will surrendered, a depth of calm and peace possessed her soul, that wonderful peace and calm which always follows on a sacrifice generously made for God. Her heroic act had instant compensation. She was rewarded by a closer degree of union with Jesus, which carried her sanctity to still greater heights. In spite of its pain, her soul was plunged in joy—the joy of possessing Jesus more closely. Her having Him did not exempt her from pain, but it excluded all sadness. God deals with us as He did with Mary; every fresh and great gift He bestows on us is but a prelude to a more pressing call on our spirit of sacrifice. He gives to us in order to prepare us to give to Him more largely.

This Mystery of the Presentation, although of such tragic intensity, is not without some light that relieves the gloom. As was said, not one of the mothers who mounted the temple steps at Mary's side realised that she was walking beside one who carried God in her arms. Not one of them saw the greatness that was veiled in that modest exterior. Yet Jesus did not pass by entirely unnoticed. In the joy that irradiated the souls of the prophet Simeon and the prophetess Anna, Mary had a glimpse of the glory and the gladness that, to men of good will, would be brought by the coming of her Son. In them she saw all those for whom He would not be a sign to be contradicted but a sign to be followed with loyalty and enthusiasm. In these two holy souls Mary saw verified the conditions which prepare the way for the discovery of God on earth. Anna, after the few years of her happy married life had sped by, gave herself up to the conquest of her flesh by a career of sustained mortification. By obliging her imagination and her thoughts to dwell day by day on God and the things of God, she had obtained a great mastery over her inner faculties. In this her soul had gained an immense freedom to devote itself to spiritual things, the animal instincts were subdued, and self-love was starved. Sternness to the flesh and resistance to the unreasonable demands of the sense life impart a great freedom of spirit and clarity of inner vision. The reward of mortification is an acuity of spiritual sight. With the subjugation of bodily passions and desires goes an intensification of the spirit of faith. Those who deny themselves valiantly see clearly in the things of God. So it proved with the prophetess Anna. She had spent long years in mortification of the flesh and in prayer. The result was that her soul responded instinctively to the presence of God. She recognised who the child was and its mother and she spoke of Him "to all that looked for the redemption of Israel."

Simeon, like Anna, had passed his life in self-denial and in the study of divine things. His self-denial took the form of detachment from and aloofness with regard to merely earthly interests. Earth had lost its grip on him. He swung free from its attractions. Valuing nothing but God, death had no terrors for him: because for him it would not mean a sundering or a snapping of ties. He wanted only one thing on earth and that was to behold with his eyes the promised redeemer. Completely detached from, and therefore soaring above earthly things, his eyes were able to discern clearly the vision he longed for when at last it presented itself to him. To the perfectly detached there is given an unblurred and undimmed vision of spiritual realities. Our vision is faulty because we wish to fix, with our regard, other things along with God. Simeon was heard beyond his desires. It was given him on earth not only to see Jesus; he was allowed to hold Jesus in his arms. At the contact his soul overflowed with peace and happiness and earth and all it contained lost all significance in his eyes, and he could say: "Now Thou dost dismiss Thy servant, O Lord, according to Thy word, in peace."

We, too, may look for the great grace that was granted Simeon. He has shown us how to prepare for and merit it. The desire of our hearts should be to see Jesus. There is only one path that will lead us to the vision. It is the way of detachment and of prayer. Prayer, according to the great St. Teresa, means a constant, loving and familiar intercourse with God. This adapts the soul for seeing Him when He shows Himself to it. The vision may be deferred for a long time for us—Simeon had to wait until age had come upon him—but if we persevere the Lord will come to us, too, some day. His mother will place Him in our arms, and a great sigh of peace and happiness and supreme contentment will be breathed forth from our soul. At that instant, earth with all its joys, its trials and its sorrows will fade away before our eyes. The world will no longer hold any attraction for us; all its ties will be snapped. Our life may not be at an end, but our life's desire will have been satisfied. We may be asked still to linger on the earth, but we shall move there as if not belonging to it, and at each moment we shall be able to repeat in our hearts those words of Simeon so filled with contentment, "Now Thou dost dismiss Thy servant, O Lord, according to Thy word, *in peace*, because my eyes have seen Thy salvation, which Thou hast prepared before the face of all peoples: a light to the revelation of the Gentiles and the glory of Thy people Israel."

C. C. MARTINDALE, S.J

THE WOMEN MARY KNEW

Even if we read all the later literature of the Jews, that is, what was written between Malachy, the last of the Prophets, and the gospels, we should still perceive ourselves to have passed into a different atmosphere, a new world, when we enter upon the New Testament. There is much that is fascinatingly interesting in that later literature, especially the "apocalyptic" or eschatological writings; in proportion as infiltrations of Greek thought modify the purely Jewish style, or indeed as Jews like Philo begin actually to write in Greek, quite new interests are aroused, though much of the Alexandrian writings is spoilt for us by not being "sincere"—their authors wanted to prove that hereditary writings were "as good as Plato" or the other Greek philosophers—indeed, that these latter had really got their lore from Moses. Hence a wearisome and quite unnatural allegorisation of the Old Testament; and continuous special pleading. No! Something had happened to the New Testament writers which had changed their minds and hearts, truly Palestinian as their temperaments remained.

It has often been pointed out that St. Matthew writes his narrative of Our Lord's childhood from St. Joseph's point of view, and indeed to me there is not much "freshness" in his style, dramatic as the episodes were. Frankly, I feel as if he were recording the episodes more because they suited his thesis—the rejection by the Jews of their prophesied Messias and the transferring of their prerogatives to the Gentiles—than because, quite simply, he loved the stories for their own sake, which you feel is what St. Luke did. No doubt St. Matthew is never a very "fresh," personal writer—not nearly so much so as either St. Mark or St. Luke (of course we possess only a translation of his original Aramaic "gospel"; even if he made the translation itself, translations are seldom quite "alive"); and probably he did not get his information first hand from St. Joseph, since it should, I think, be accepted that Joseph had died before the beginning of Our Lord's ministry, so Matthew may never have known him. On the other hand, the "childhood" stories of St. Luke are simply redolent with a sweet, fresh air; nay, what is more, while his personal style holds good throughout both Gospel and Acts, there is a slight difference in it during these first chapters; elsewhere, I think you feel that his considerable general culture had slightly "educated" his Palestinianism: here, there is, without any loss of dignity, a certain naiveness; a sweetness, as we said; and yet a Biblical grandeur that comes straight from the Old Testament. The upshot is that we hold (and I believe that an increasing number of scholars now admit) that Luke, that earnest seeker for first-hand evidence (1:1–4), obtained his information as to Our Lord's childhood straight from the lips of Mary.

Impossible to dwell on details: and, anyhow, as the stories are well known, let them but be re-read with this in mind—that Our Lady herself is relating these mysteries to you; without the waste of a word; with that humility which never is false; and in those forms which show how her whole mind had been fashioned by the Holy Scriptures, her inheritance.

The Annunciation reached her mind wholly in that phrasing: during the exquisite episode of the Visitation (to which she went "with haste") the Magnificat was sung in such a way as to recall at once the psalm sung by Anna, Samuel's mother (though to me, quite as strongly, Psalm 107)— and yet who can possibly fail to taste the difference?

Put it thus—had the songs been interchanged, and had Anna's song been assigned to Mary, would we not have felt sorry? And, in fact, that Mary *could* not possibly have sung just *that*? We treasure the memory of St. Elizabeth—the Rosary reminds us daily of her: perhaps that other Anna (Luke 2:36) appears too briefly for us often to think of her, though St. Luke is able to base her personality very firmly—he gives her father's name; her tribe; how long she had lived with her husband; that she was a widow of eighty-four years. She was "always in the Temple"; she was continuously praying and fasting; she came upon them "just at the right moment," recognized Messias in the Child, and proceeded to speak of Him to all who were awaiting the ransom of the People.

I cannot believe that she and Elizabeth and Mary never met again! Old women are always fond of a very young mother; perhaps Mary's own mother was still alive. Here is almost a new picture—Mary, amid these aged women, so perfectly modest among them, so always God's little handmaid; yet they must have been absorbed in the spiritual loveliness that radiated unconsciously from her soul.

Not but what their more general disbelief must have made things very difficult for Mary within her nearer circle of relatives, especially as it is clear that they asked her to side with them, and to check Our Lord in His preaching; and Salome at least accompanied John and James—if she did not actually egg them on!—when they made their request for the two chief posts in their Master's future "government." Mary must have suffered to some degree, by thus companioning her kinsfolk,[1] even though on the occasion of the second visit, she must have heard that in the densely thronged house He had not room so much as to eat.... That would have troubled any mother!

But outside that circle I suppose that her closest friend must have been the Magdalen. Mary the Magdalen will have needed friends more than anyone, and it has often seemed to me an outstanding proof of Our Lord's trust in and appreciation of His Mother, that He should not only have allowed but manifestly been pleased with that association, and it will not have been without His special goodwill that the Immaculate Virgin and the Magdalen were so close together beneath the Cross.

---

1.   It is not certain who Our Lord's cousins were. Was Our Lady aunt of the hot-headed young John and James, sons of Zebedee? I used to think: "probably." Now I do not think so. But I think that she was, of "James and Joseph"; and possibly, though not probably, of Simon and Jude. This very technical matter cannot be discussed here, nor is it of any importance that it should be. The point is that Our Lord had many "kinsfolk," and what He said would happen at large, happened within His own "family." Some believed in Him; others did not. What is certain, from tradition, is, that Mary had no children other than Our Lord: and Scripture itself makes the same thing so "morally certain" that we can accept the fact from that source also. What is insisted on here is the suffering of Mary due to the fact that "to His own He came," and that by no means all of "His own" accepted Him.

CARYLL HOUSELANDER

LITANY TO OUR LADY

Lady, giver of Bread,
Christ-bestowing,
give us the Bread of Life!

Fallow land for the sowing,
darkness over the seed,
secrecy for the growing;
give us the Living Bread.

Empty cup for the wine,
white linen, spread
without fold for the feast:
give us the Bread of Heaven,
yeast and leaven,
Christ-bestowing:
give us to eat.
Give us the Bread in the wheat,
Lady, giver of Bread.

Full grape in the vine,
give us the strong Wine
poured into the chalice
and lifted up.

Drained cup,
give us the broken Bread;
give us the crust of sorrow,
hard as rye,
Christ-bestowing.

Give us the emptiness
of the dark furrow,
while the great wind
of the Spirit is blowing
and sowing seed.

Lady, giver of Bread,
field sown by the wind,
snow white on the field,
darkness under the snow:
yield
the Bread of Life!

Wheat, leaven and yeast
and wine for the feast:
give us the Bread of Life,

Lady, giver of Bread,
Christ-bestowing.

C. C. MARTINDALE, S.J

༄ ༄

THE FIRST THREE SORROWS

Eve, so named because she was "Mother of all living" (Gen. 3:20), became for that very reason Mother too of all who should die. When—the first Mater Dolorosa—she held upon her knees the murdered body of her son Abel, she stood at the head of a long history of Death, which, so far as human bodies go, is not even yet completed. Indeed, Abel was seeming to her just then her only son; for though Cain was alive, he had fled; she could not see him: she knew nothing save that he was "in the land of wandering." As for Cain, he foresaw well enough that he had originated a tale of vengeance—"whosoever findeth me, shall kill me!"

But even for him, in the hour of his despair, God provided at least this consolation—he and his race should not be exterminated: nay, on anyone who should kill him, vengeance should be wreaked "sevenfold." Yet alas, even this became the occasion for a sneer and for new blood-thirstiness in that tainted race. His descendant Lameck made a song—

As for me, I will slay a man for merely wounding me!
Yes, a young man for so much as bruising me!

If Cain shall be avenged seven-fold,
Then Lamech, seven and seventy-fold!

And ever since there has been in our wretched world a race of the violent and the outcast—of Cains, and Ishmaels, and Esaus.

But to Eve a better consolation was appointed. She bore another son, and called him *Seth*, exclaiming: "God hath given [or assigned] me another seed instead of Abel," for *Seth* is assonant to the word *scith*, "assigned." So once more Eve became Mother of the Living.

Life, Death, and Life may be said to be the history of Mary, too, albeit there was no sin in her.

You may say that Our Lady's self-sacrificial life began when she made (as we cannot but believe that she did) her decision to remain virgin. This certainly involved, for her, the renunciation of any hope that she should be Mother of the Messias. The prophecy of Isaias did not create or perhaps even witness to a general tradition that the Messias should be born of a Virgin.[1] The humble child experienced the inspiration thus to dedicate herself wholly to God, and, obedient as ever, as ever His hand-maiden "whose eyes are upon the hands of her mistress," she listened to the heavenly prompting and was content to wait, to hope and to pray, and would have given the most unselfish homage to the Messias's Mother, should she have been allowed, some day, to meet her. She was happy in her self-sacrifice: but it *was* a "whole burnt-offering"

---

1. It is true that Revelation, before Christ, as after Him, need not have been confined to those utterances that are preserved in the Scriptures. We possess but scant fragments of what the prophets said. But in the absence of any evidence whatsoever, we cannot assume that there *was* another stream of tradition or popular belief to the effect that the Messias should be virgin-born, or even that there was any popular esteem for virginity at all.

of herself and her future that she made. No more extreme instance of so losing one's life that one finds it!

The episode of the Visitation must have been one of pure ecstasy: but, had it not been that Mary "waited" thus "upon the Lord," and interposed no conditions of her own upon the sequence of events, the period of St. Joseph's bewilderment must have been agony, and even Bethlehem a very shadowed joy, seeing that she can hardly but have felt that He had "come to His own, and His own received Him not."

FIRST SORROW

But, with that alternation of pain and consolation which, we saw, was God's method from the outset, the Presentation in the Temple made up for that, at least for a moment. Ample, indeed manifestly miraculous, was Simeon's recognition and acceptance of the Child he took up into his arms: how, amid all that throng, could he have singled out the working-man and his young wife and her Baby, save by divine illumination? And magnificent indeed was the prophecy of his Psalm! But at once the shadow fell again. Turning to Mary herself, he said:

> This Child is set to bring about the fall, as well as the upris-
> ing, of many in Israel—to be a Sign, but a Sign that shall be
> contradicted—that so the thoughts of many hearts may be
> revealed—yes, and thine own soul a sword shall pierce!

We have placed Simeon's parenthesis after the words that follow it in St. Luke for clearness' sake. Simeon had most clearly foretold the

169

Messiah-hood of Mary's Son—that He should be a light for the Gentiles no less than a Glory for the Jews. But His victory was to be no more than partial. Not all would receive that Light nor walk in it. While some should rise and stand upright because of Him, others should fall because of Him, and thus should be revealed that most mysterious thing—the innermost "set" of the soul, obscure till some shock or challenge brings it to light: St. Luke's word *dialogismoi* means more than "thoughts"; it means the whole mental movement; the putting this against that and the assessing of the result: the Child could not but become a Sign, something set up high and inevitably noticed; but some would say this about it, some that. In a thousand ways Mary's heart should be pierced as by a sword: her love for her people, which was God's people; her anguish when she should watch them rejecting their Saviour: her love for her Son and her desire to see Him universally triumphant; and, her resignation to God's Will, which did not intend to coerce human wills so as to ensure that universal triumph: her longing that her little Child should be happy, and, her perception, ever growing, that He was marked for Martyrdom; yes, and that she, inseparable from Him, would have to share in that which we now know to have been Calvary.

SECOND SORROW

The months went by (perhaps a year or more)—a breathing-space. Then came the strange joy of the Magi's visit, followed forthwith by the news that in direct consequence of that visit Herod was seeking the Child's life. The Holy Family fled: true, Egypt was not far—its northern part was full of Jews who even had a sort of model temple there. Mary and

Joseph would have found their own talk, customs, and compatriots. And they were safe. But apart from the tormenting anxiety of the actual flight, and the heartbreak due to the murder of the Innocents of which echoes may easily have reached her, it must have seemed bewildering to Mary that already the "Sign" was being spoken against—humanly speaking, everything seemed to be going wrong. Even when Herod died, and they felt safe in returning to Bethlehem (where I think Joseph had meant to go on living), they were too frightened to stay there once they heard that Herod Archelaus had inherited Judea. He was a worse monster even than his father. So they returned to Nazareth.

Even there life was no suave idyll. When Jesus was about ten, the turbulent north-country Galileans made a raid on an armoury of Herod Antipas at Sepphoris, visible from the hillcrest over Nazareth. The Romans, to make an example, crucified two thousand men of that townlet and the neighbourhood. Jesus and Mary must have been accustomed throughout their lives to the sight of men dying upon crosses.

THIRD SORROW

But a true turning-point was imminent. Jesus seems to dissociate Himself from these two souls who loved Him so dearly. The Holy Family went yearly to Jerusalem for the Pasch. Jesus was now twelve years old—on the eve of coming of age. When the caravan returned, He was not to be found. The first stage of such a pilgrimage is said to have been short: next morning, therefore, they were back in Jerusalem, hunting in anguish for Him. Not till the next day did they find Him under the Temple colonnades where Rabbis held classes and taught the Scriptures to children.

And there was Jesus, listening and asking questions. When they on their side catechised Him, "they were all of them out of themselves" at the intelligence shown by His answers. But when his parents saw Him, they were thunderstruck, and Mary said: "Son, why have you done so to us? Your father and I have sought you in anguish!" But He said: "How was it that you sought me? Did you not know that I must be—it was my duty to be—in my Father's house?"[2] "Thy father and I?" No: *God* was His Father. The house at Nazareth? No: His native home was *God's* house— the Temple.

---

2.   In the Douay version: "about my Father's business." The Greek might mean either.

EDWARD LEEN, C.S.SP.

ᘒ ᘒ

THE MIRACLE AT CANA

St. John is the only one of the Evangelists who transmits to us the story of the incidents that marked the marriage feast at Cana of Galilee. He narrates the event in great detail. He notes apparently trivial circumstances, as, for instance, the procedure of the waiters, the number of the water-pots, their capacity and finally the remarks made on the quality of the wine by the master of the feast. To St. John, writing in his old age and looking back over the long series of years that had passed, and analysing the gradual development of the Church, the happenings at this marriage, an ordinary event in the social life of the Jews, had a significance that escaped the minds of the other inspired historians of the life of the Saviour. For them probably the miracle at the marriage was but one miracle among many others, less striking than most, perhaps, and certainly not containing any elements that would invest it with a special importance. This is not surprising. Those who live close to historical events cannot see them in their true perspective nor can they mark their bearing on other happenings which with them constitute an important cycle in the history of mankind. St. John was much better circumstanced than the others, to see the great importance that this miracle of the changing of the water into wine had as revealing and stressing a factor of the highest significance in the economy of the redemption of mankind. The chosen disciple had lived for many years after the crucifixion with Mary, the Mother of Jesus: he had seen the influence she exercised on the growth of the Church and in the distribution of graces that contributed to that growth. In the light of this experience he saw and understood the meaning of the combination of circumstances that attended the miracle at Cana. He saw why it was not wrought by Jesus through a sentiment of pity for a suffering revealed to Him by the sufferers themselves, as in all other cases. Of all the miracles in the Gospel this is the only one in which Mary intervenes. St. John grasped the full import of this intervention. He saw why it was pre-ordained that this intervention should take place. It shed light for him on the whole economy of the Redemption. In that light stood revealed to his spiritual vision the place of Mary in that scheme of divine mercy. The mode of the miracle manifested clearly to him the active part that falls to the lot of "the Woman" in the working out of the salvation of mankind. In the fact that Mary had with Jesus her definite part to play in the accomplishment of the marvellous change of water into wine, St. John traced the working out of the primeval prophecy which linked for ever and inseparably "the Woman" with her seed in the work of the restoration of mankind: how God had said to the serpent that He would place enmities between him and the Woman, between his seed and her seed: and how the serpent's head should be crushed (Gen. 3:15). It was at Mary's word—the word of "the Woman"—that was, for the first time, unloosed the divine power of which Satan was presently to feel the effects and the manifestations of which would be the first indication to him of the approaching collapse of his empire. Understanding clearly in the light of subsequent events and in virtue of his prophetic insight, that the peculiar significance of the miracle at Cana lay not only in its being a showing forth of the divine power of Jesus, but also in its revelation of the *rôle* of Mary as cooperating in the work of her Son, St. John dwells on it in a very expressive manner. Having completed his narrative of the events that transpired at the feast, he underlines the fact that no miracle had, in the life of the Saviour, preceded this one of the changing of water into wine. "This *beginning of miracles* did Jesus in Cana of Galilee and manifested His glory" (John 2:2). Having occasion somewhat later on in his narrative to make mention of Cana, his mind again reverts to the miracle that took place at the marriage feast. "*He came again therefore into Cana of Galilee, where he made the water wine*" (John 4:46).

In itself, as a work of power, this miracle at Cana is not to be compared with other wonders related by the fourth Evangelist, as for instance, the raising of Lazarus from the tomb; yet it is clear that it was for St. John one marked with characteristics that singled it out and gave it a place apart from all the others. In the light of ancient prophecy and in the experience of the actual fulfillment of these prophecies in the gradual evolution of the Church, St. John understood that the wonder wrought at Cana was invested with a special supernatural significance belonging to none of the other miracles. These were done to prove the divinity of Jesus or to show that the seal of the divine approval was set on His teaching: the incident at Cana over and above this purpose had that of revealing the essential part that Mary, the Mother of Jesus, plays in the economy of the Redemption, and the providential place that she occupies in the life of the Church.

It is remarkable that whilst, on the whole, the life and actions of Mary are left in profound obscurity by the sacred writers, this obscurity is not unbroken by flashes of light. She is, at times, given prominence by the Evangelists and invariably at what may be called the pivotal moments in the life of the Saviour. What is more, when she does appear, it is always with full light thrown on her, the other actors in these scenes (except, of course, her Divine Child) standing in comparative shadow. On each occasion she is the central figure. The attention of the reader is necessarily fixed on her. She dominates the situation. Even in the presence of the great Archangel Gabriel, during the whole of that momentous dialogue on which turned the destinies of mankind, the eyes, as it were, are fixed and the attention of all ages focussed on the face of the Virgin. It is clearly understood that it is her word that will determine the denouement of this most dramatic situation in the history of mankind since the Fall. The brilliant archangel, as a dignified but yet obsequious messenger, moves on the outward rim of that strong circle of light in which is thrown into powerful relief the figure of the maiden of Nazareth.[1] When the hour of the Nativity comes, it is Mary, who, unaided by any human helpers, gives the Saviour to mankind and who on mankind's behalf offers the immediate ministrations that the helpless infant needs. St. Joseph is there: he is the master of the household, but still he remains in the dim and shadowy background. "And it came to pass when they were there, her days were accomplished that she should be delivered. And she brought forth her first-born Son, and wrapped him up in swaddling clothes and laid Him in a manger." When the shepherds came in haste to see "Christ the Lord" whose birth had been announced to them,

---

1. One has but to contrast this scene with all others in Scripture in which angels appear to men. The difference is striking and obvious. No matter how great and holy be the human being who is favoured with the presence of the heavenly visitant, it is the person of God's messenger that dominates the situation.

it is not stated simply that they found the child, but that "they found Mary and Joseph and the Infant lying in a manger." And lest this might be thought to be a characteristic of St. Luke and due to the special devotedness to the Virgin, which tradition attributes to him, there is the same note in the narrative of St. Matthew. Narrating the arrival of the three kings, he says: "And entering the house, they *found the Child with Mary His Mother.* And falling down they adored Him." It is as if the Evangelists were inspired to represent the Virgin in the attitude of holding forth and presenting the Saviour to the whole Gentile world, present in the person of these three wise men. There is no mention of the foster-father of Jesus in the scene. And yet immediately afterwards when there is question of protecting the life of the Child and saving Him from a pressing danger, it is St. Joseph to whom the angel appears, and it is St. Joseph who is the chief actor in the tragic flight into Egypt. "And after they were departed, behold an angel of the Lord appeared in sleep to Joseph saying: Arise and take the Child and His mother and fly into Egypt, and be there until I shall tell thee; he arose and took the Child and His mother by night and retired into Egypt." "But when Herod was dead, behold an angel of the Lord appeared *in sleep* to Joseph in Egypt saying: Arise, and take the Child and His mother and go into the land of Israel. But hearing that Archelaus reigned in Judea...*he* was afraid to go thither; and being warned in sleep retired into the quarters of Galilee. And coming he dwelt in a city called Nazareth." It is interesting to observe how naturally the person of the foster-father of Jesus assumes, in vigorous and decisive actions, the chief *rôle* throughout the whole of this episode. When it is a question of preserving Jesus for His life-work it is Joseph who holds the principal place, but when it is a question of that life-work itself, then it is that Mary steps into prominence. That she is necessarily involved in, and has a definite part to fulfil in the work of breaking the power of Satan and redeeming mankind, is unmistakably stressed in the totally unexpected sequel to the Presentation in the Temple, after the forty days of the Purification had rolled by. These six weeks of bliss were for Mary a pathetic preparation for what awaited her when Joseph and herself had carried out the requirements of the Mosaic Law in regard to the child. The devout Simeon, filled with the prophetic spirit, took the Infant in his arms and said to *Mary His Mother*: "Behold this child is set for the fall and for the redemption of many in Israel and for a sign which shall be contradicted. And thy own soul a sword shall pierce, that, out of many hearts, thoughts may be revealed." It is not possible to read these words without being filled with pity for the young mother, who was thus tragically enlightened as to the fate that awaited the child. Yet there was some comfort—even if a bitter comfort—for the heart of the mother in the prophet's words. The fate of the child was a tragic one: yet he would not be alone in enduring it. It was unmistakably shown that the mother herself should share the child's fate and be caught up in the same tragic destiny. The logical sequence of Simeon's phrases clearly reveals that an indissoluble link bound Mary and Jesus together in the great struggle which was to issue in the undoing of the primeval curse. "Behold this child is set for a sign which shall be contradicted...and thy own soul a sword shall pierce." The great contradiction was to envelop them both. The Passion of the Child was to have as its counterpart the compassion of the mother. Here again Mary is the central and the tragic figure. The light is turned full on her. There is not a word addressed to St. Joseph nor is there any mention of his name. He had no part to play in the great drama which the prophecy dimly and in outline foreshadowed. Again, when the days of childhood had passed and Jesus, for reasons that are for us inscrutable, but which certainly had a bearing on His Messianic mission, withdrew Himself from His parents for three days, it is Mary, not Joseph, who addressed Him a loving remonstrance after their agonising search had ended by finding the boy in the Temple conversing with the doctors of the law. "And seeing Him they wondered. And His mother said to Him: Son, why hast thou done so to us? Behold thy father and I have sought Thee sorrowing." The reply and the actions of Jesus were enigmatic for both his parents. The actions appeared to contradict the words. He said to them: "How is it that you sought me? Did you not know that I must be about my Father's business?" (Luke 5:49). By logical implication these words would seem to signify an intention on the part of Jesus to persevere in some course on which He had embarked and a denial of the right of His parents to seek Him out and withhold Him from it. On the other hand, He assents to Mary's implied request that He should return with herself and Joseph to the shelter of their home in Nazareth. He seems to oppose and yet to comply with her desires. "And he went down with them and came to Nazareth and was subject to them" (Luke 2:51). Mary not being given at this moment insight into the meaning of this mysterious occurrence, turned it over constantly, in all its details, in her mind, striving to probe its depths. "And His mother kept all these words in her heart" (Luke 5:52). Did the light dawn on her eighteen years later when there took place another event which constituted a close parallel to this one of the Three Days' Loss and its sequel? *Did she understand that, as it was in the plan of Divine Providence that her prayer should inaugurate the public life of her Divine Son, so also was it decided that her gentle pleading should close the door on that mysterious hidden life* that was to be the divinely ordained preparation for the Three Years' Ministry? It was at the prayer of "The Woman" that were disposed the different parts of the scheme by which the redemption was to be worked out, as it was by the words and actions of "another woman" that was determined the course of events that precipitated the downfall of mankind. The incident at Cana is but an instance of the prevalent antithesis between Mary and Eve. Mary's Fiat, at the Annunciation, gave Jesus to men; her gentle complaint secured the long years of seclusion and preparation for combat; her request at Cana inaugurates the life of conflict; and finally, on Calvary the redemptive sacrifice was not accomplished until she had signified her acceptance of that sacrifice and surrendered her child to death on behalf of mankind.

It is worthy of note that it was not, apparently, on His own account but on account of His mother that Jesus was present at the wedding festivities at Cana. It is very likely that were her presence not looked for by the bridal couple, He would not have been there. It was to Mary that the invitation had been issued in the first instance. "And the third day there was a marriage in Cana of Galilee: *and the Mother of Jesus was there.*" Most probably she was asked to the feast because of some relationship between her and the wedded pair, and because her practical help and advice would be needed in the arrangements to be made for the festivities. A woman of her years, experience and capacity would be of invaluable assistance on an occasion of the kind. After having mentioned that the mother of Jesus was present, St. John continues, saying: "*And Jesus also* was invited and His disciples to the marriage." The logical sequence shows that the disciples were bidden to the feast out of compliment to their Master and the Master Himself out of compliment to His Mother. Mary is the door by which the Saviour enters on His public career. As the feasting progressed it began to appear that, as often happens in households when unusual numbers are gathered together, a miscalculation had been made. The supplies provided for the guests began to run short. Mary, who, most probably, had had a hand in the preparations and arrangements, was the first to perceive the menace of an awkward and, for the young spouses, a humiliating situation. Her woman's sympathy and solicitude were aroused. How was the danger, she asked herself, to be averted?

We who read the narrative in the light of subsequent events, and are influenced by the knowledge thereby acquired, take it as being a very normal and natural thing that Mary should in her difficulty turn to her Son and ask for a miracle. The occasion seems to us to call for this. And yet a little reflection suffices to show that her action was a complete departure from what had been the customary in her relations with Jesus. For thirty years she had lived with her Son and during all that time nothing but everyday human means had been taken to cope with the necessities that arose from time to time. By daily toil the needs of the household had been supplied. Frequently, at Nazareth, there would be the usual interchange of good offices between neighbours—the customary mutual borrowings and lendings to meet special and transient necessities. There had never been any manifestations of divine power. In the present crisis the normal thing for Mary would have been to enlist the services of kindly neighbours to save the situation. Yet she does not do this, but turned to her Son, saying, "They have no wine."

What moved Mary to take this step? Did she look to her Son to perform a miracle to save her friends from the embarrassing situation in which they found themselves? She had never seen her Son exercising any miraculous power: she had never known Him to apply anything but the obvious human means to meet and solve the difficulties that life continually presents. Nothing she had experienced during the thirty years prepared her for a departure from what had been the habitual mode of procedure. Yet, moved by an instinct of the Holy Ghost, she addressed herself to Jesus, confident that, somehow—very likely she was not quite clear as to what steps would actually be taken—Jesus would do something to meet the difficulty. She expected that something would happen—she knew not what. All that was definite was her perfect confidence that her anxiety on behalf of her friends would be relieved. It is not fanciful to detect a slight similarity between her state of mind and that of Andrew, the brother of Peter, on the occasion of the first multiplication of loaves. When Philip, in reply to a question of the Master, had stated that a very costly supply of bread was needed to satisfy the wants of the crowd that followed them, Andrew intervened, saying: "There is a boy here that hath five barley loaves and two fishes: but what are these among so many?" (John 6:9). There is a great deal conveyed in that adversative conjunction, "*but.*" One can visualise the gesture of the hands and the expression of the countenance that accompanied it. In the light of the psychology of human intercourse, it is clear what was the state of mind of Andrew on this occasion. Whilst acknowledging the obvious fact that five barley loaves and two fishes could avail nothing towards satisfying the multitude, yet his making mention of them at all, and his drawing attention in the same breath to their insufficiency, manifested that in his secret soul he trusted that in some indefinable way the Master could with this small supply parry the situation that presented itself. In a somewhat similar fashion Mary on this occasion knew perfectly well that Jesus had neither money nor means to command an immediate supply of wine—yet she trusted Him to find a way out of the impasse. She does not ask for a miracle: she simply lays bare a pressing need, and leaves the rest to His discretion. This is an admirable way of praying. One merely exposes the wants of one's soul before the Lord and having unfolded them before Him, one expectantly and confidently fixes the gaze of the spirit on the divine countenance. The unformed and unphrased petition is more eloquent than the most perfectly phrased discourse.

Mary's touching and mute appeal is met, apparently, with a rebuff. Jesus said to her: "*Woman*, what is it to me and to thee? My hour is not yet come." The words are strange and mysterious, but not more mysterious than the ones pronounced eighteen years previously in the Temple. At that time, as is expressly stated by the inspired writer, the words of Jesus were not understood by His mother. They gave her food for deep and constant thought. Now, on this occasion, there is no hint given that she failed to grasp the meaning underlying her Son's rejoinder. On the contrary, everything that ensued demonstrates that she clearly seized what the answer to her unspoken petition involved, how it would be granted and *the principle of action* behind Jesus' strange way of assenting to her request.

There is neither harshness nor disrespect in the words of the Saviour. "Woman" is a title of honour and reverence and has the same force as that mode of address so frequent in Greek tragedies—O Gynai, that is, Lady or Mistress. "What is it to me and to thee" is an expression that occurs frequently in Sacred Scripture both in the Old and in the New Testament.[2] Whilst having in all cases the same meaning substantially, this meaning is invested with varied "nuances," according to circumstances, such as the tone of voice of the speaker, the situation which calls forth the remark, the emotion the speaker is suffering from and the rest. Taking the residue of meaning which is left, after abstracting from all

---

2. Judges 11:12; 3 Kings 17:18; 4 Kings 7:13; Luke 8:28.

these accidental differences the sense seems to be something like this. He who employs this peculiarly oriental locution wishes to convey to his interlocutor that the grounds on which the latter is basing or intends to base a certain course of action, and which, in his opinion, justify such a course, either do not exist at all or, if they exist, do not justify the action taken or intended to be taken. The party that utters the remonstrance says in effect to the other: "You are doing (or as the case may be, are about to do or have done) an action, and you judge yourself entitled to do so on certain grounds: in actual fact you are wrong in acting as you do, because the grounds do not exist or are not of such a nature as to leave you blameless if you take this course." The words have always a note of remonstrance. But the remonstrance bears on the principle of action primarily, and by way of consequence only on the action itself. Hence it is that it implies a refusal—though not necessarily. The words ordinarily imply a refusal, because, if the reasons which are thought to exist for taking certain steps do not really exist, then, of course, these steps should not be taken. But if the speaker insinuates that, though the grounds of action erroneously considered to be present are not really present, still there are other grounds discoverable which could justify the action in question, then the words do not intimate a refusal, but the necessity for a change in the principle of action.

This is the situation at the feast of Cana. Mary, listening only to the promptings of her tender interest in and pity for the awkward situation in which her friends are placed, and accustomed to the docility of her Son where her wishes are concerned, approaches Him as she was wont to do during the thirty years of the hidden life. Without expressly asking for a miracle, she implicitly does so. For her unspoken request could not be granted without a miracle. Up to that moment the *motive* that moved Jesus in all the actions He did for His mother was *deference* to that mother's wishes—deference to her, who, as His Mother, had the right to direct and order His doings. But in the few days since He had emerged from the obscurity of Nazareth a definite change in their relations had taken place. Obedience to His Mother was the principle of the actions of His home life. Miracles belonged to His public life. In the public life the controlling and directing influence postulating obedience on His part—belonged to His *Heavenly* Father, not to His earthly Mother. A miracle was part of the being about "His Father's business" and could be wrought only at the time, place, occasion and in the circumstances determined from all eternity by God, His Father. "My hour is not yet come," He said. He meant the hour marked in the eternal decrees. The shortage of wine had become acute. It was the perception of that shortage that moved Mary to speak. Jesus perceived it on the instant it had become apparent to the servants. This knowledge of the acute want does not stir Him to action. The hour of need—that is, the moment when the need was felt—was not the hour of Divine Providence. Some other circumstance distinct from the need and over and above was required if Jesus was to act. *That circumstance was the intervention of Mary.* When that intervention had taken place the hour decided on from all eternity had come.

A ray of divine light revealed all this to the Mother of the Saviour when His words ceased to sound in her ears. She grasped the change that had taken place. When she had begun to address Him, it had been in the old manner. *When His words ended she knew that her request was not refused but granted in entirely new conditions.* She realised that the words of her Son were not to her dishonour but to her exceeding great honour. It flashed on her in an instant that though she could not *command* a miracle as Mother, the miracle would, nevertheless, be conceded to her as all-powerful intercessor. She understood, in the instant, that the hour marked in the Divine Decree for the intervention of that all-powerful intercession of hers had now sounded. It stood revealed to her that the Almighty in His eternal regard for her linked indissolubly the inauguration of her Son's public career with her prayers. As the decree of the Incarnation hung on her Fiat, so the decree of the miracle that ushered in the life of Power of the Incarnate God was suspended to her words of intercession. The "hour of Jesus" had not come, having regard to the mode in which Mary began her petition—that is, in regard to the ideas of things which were in her mind when she said: "They have no wine"—the hour had come if regard be had to the enlightenment as to her *rôle* in the economy of redemption, that was imparted to her at the words of Jesus. The hour had not come (to use a theological formula) "in *sensu composito*" with the idea which Mary had, at the outset, of the part that fell to her to play in saving the situation at the feast: it had come "*in sensu composito*" with the knowledge that was given her of the part of tremendous import

---

3.   Regarded from the point of view of time, a scarcely measurable space elapsed between the moment when the hour was not yet come, and that when it had come. But there had taken place a considerable change in moral and spiritual relations. In the *Vie de N. S. Jésus Christ* by L. de Fillion (vol. 2, p. 97), we read: "Only a very short space of time had elapsed between Mary's order to the servants and the words of Jesus to her; but according to a very profound remark a change in moral and spiritual conditions is not measured by lapse of time. At the moment that Jesus spoke to His Mother the hour had not come. In the instant after, when her soul was enlightened by His words as to the part she had to play in the miracle and the attitude she should have towards Him in regard to His public life, the hour had come. There is a parallel situation exposed in the seventh chapter of St. John's Gospel, when Jesus said to His brethren: 'Go you up to this festival day: but I go not up to this festival day, because my time is not accomplished.' But then immediately after we are told: 'After His brethren were gone up, then He also went up to the feast, not openly, but as it were in secret.' He was not going up after the manner in which that going up was linked, in the minds of His brethren, with

that was actually hers in this incident.[3] Her real part in this miracle was one that her humility had hidden from her until the moment that, with her Son's words, came the illumination of the Holy Ghost, disclosing the inner meaning of things. It stood revealed to her that the miracle was due to her in her capacity of "Omnipotent Suppliant."

That Mary perfectly understood this time and was not at a loss, as at the Finding in the Temple, is evidenced by her prompt and decisive action. It is to be noted that it is not Jesus but she that speaks to the servants, in the first instance. She becomes the central figure—always excepting, of course, her Divine Son. She issues commands as being mistress of the situation. She was perfectly instructed by the Holy Ghost as to the fact that her request had been granted and as to the grounds on which it was granted. She was enlightened, too, as to what should be

---

a self-advertising display of power. He was going up if regard be had to the manner of going up, i.e., in an unostentatious way. that He contemplated in His own mind. He was not going in one sense: in another sense and after other principles than those which existed in the minds of His relatives, He was going."

4.   The Venerable F. M. P. Libermann, C.S.Sp., whose analysis of this incident in his commentary on the Gospel of St. John has been, with slight modifications, followed, writes: "The text may be explained in the following manner. The guests did not take Jesus for the Son of God but for a man inspired by God.... In His actions they saw the man only and believed that He acted out of love and obedience to His Mother, whereas in all that concerns His ministry and even during the whole time that He exercised it, He had no longer any relations of obedience to His Mother. For all that regarded His hidden life, it could be said of Him: He was subject to them, but for all that concerns His public life, He received orders only from His Heavenly Father directly and took action only in accordance with the eternal determinations that had been taken and decreed by His Father with regard to all His actions, and as to the time and manner in which they were to be done.... Therefore it is as if Jesus said to His Mother, 'To tell me, as being my Mother, that I ought to begin to work miracles, that does not enter into your function as Mother. You have not, as I have, read from all eternity in the bosom of the Father, His decrees on my works of grace. It is for Him to order and I ought to execute His orders directly....' At the same time that Jesus spoke these words either to instruct His Mother at the beginning of His ministry or thereby to enlighten the attendants He addressed His Mother in different wise in the interior of her heart. He made her to understand the

done preparatory to the working of this great miracle.[4]

This changing of water into wine is the first of that long series of benefits that mankind has obtained from the providence of God through the intervention of the Blessed Virgin Mary. These benefits belong to the natural as well as to the supernatural order. She has a heart full of sympathy for all the sorrows and miseries that afflict the children of Adam. She is not one who is alive only to ills of a moral and spiritual nature, whilst remaining insensible to those which are of a purely temporal kind. She is ready to succour men even in their temporal necessities, but in so doing she aims at making her beneficent actions a means of drawing souls to her Divine Son. Her function is to distribute to men the benefits of the redemption and thereby secure their happiness. It is for this she labours. It is the part in the work of salvation that has from all eternity been assigned to her by God. The Almighty having once determined to give the Redeemer to man by the Immaculate Virgin, the plan of the imparting of the Divine Gifts never undergoes a change. Mankind having obtained through her the inexhaustible fountain of all grace, continues to receive through her intervention all the different applications of that grace, as well in the temporal realm as in the spiritual. It is impossible to use terms which exaggerate the power of the intercession of Mary on behalf of mankind. She holds the key of the Divine treasury—that treasury that is filled to overflowing with the merits of her Divine Son. To her care is committed the distribution of the contents of the treasury. It is her

---

designs of God, showed her that her request had been granted, and taught her that God, having regard for her holy Prayers, had out of the great love He bore her inaugurated the hour of His miracles and His teaching. Mary, pierced through with the arrows of love that came from the heart of Jesus, made aware of her son's acquiescence to her pleading, *seeing clearly the greatness of God's designs on her...*bade the servants do as her Son should tell them."

prayer that unlocks it. Her Son cannot refuse her anything. Her love for man, so far from being diminished by her elevation to Heaven, acquires, on the contrary, a greater perfection. To secure men's welfare, temporal and spiritual, she will leave nothing untried that lies within the vast limits of the Divine Will concerning the children of Adam. She never hesitates to demand any grace, whatsoever it be, compatible with the known intentions of God. These intentions as regards the human race are fully revealed to her, as being Mother of the Redeemer and called upon with Him to co-operate in the work of redemption. Her power over the heart of God always remains a power of intercession. But she has in a certain sense a right that her intercession should be favourably received. "Because the Incarnate God is Son of Mary, and it is the duty of every son to cherish his mother, what is liberality on His part towards others becomes an obligation as regards the Virgin Mary."[5] The right that the Mother of Jesus has to be loved by Him involves a right to have her prayers heard and her desires fulfilled.

---

5.   Bossuet, 3rd Sermon on the Nativity of the Blessed Virgin Mary.

CHARLES JOURNET

THE TRIAL OF SEPARATION

When death comes to take away a child there is heartbreak. But when the mother can have pride in her son, when she hears that he died in a desperate attack or for a noble cause, she finds consolation in the praises that wreathe his memory. Her sorrow is not an unmixed grieving.

But if with her own eyes she sees her son mocked, beaten, spit upon, what is there that can lighten her suffering? In such a moment she will ask one favour only, to be allowed to be near her son to protect him with her tenderness. This favour our Lady was not granted. And it was her Son who refused it.

The episode is in the third chapter of St. Mark's gospel. Jesus had chosen his apostles. He had driven out demons and had begun to preach the Kingdom of God. Crowds thronged about Him. He entered a house. The crowds gathered there likewise, so that they could not even take their food. "And when His friends had heard of it, they went out to lay hold on Him. For it was said: He is become mad. And the scribes who were come down from Jerusalem said: He hath Beelzebub and by the prince of devils he casteth out devils."

Thus the scribes looked upon Jesus as one possessed; but many thought He was merely mad. "They said," or, "It was said: He is become mad." Who said this? Not His relations, presumably. Certainly not His Mother. But His relations and still more His Mother were anxious. They knew that He was alone, exposed to the ill-will of the people and the hatred of the scribes. For that cause they came.

Poor Mother! She knew the bite of a new sort of suffering. Up till now it had not occurred to her that the salvation of the world required that her Son, who was Wisdom Incarnate, should be treated like a madman and that He in whom the word of God dwelt ineffably should be accused of being possessed by Beelzebub. These insults, these blasphemies were a new note in her heart's agony. She knew that her Son felt them likewise and that His heart was bleeding under them. For she knew that within the house, where the scribes had come, He sought to justify Himself before them: "How can Satan cast out Satan? And if a kingdom be divided against itself, that kingdom cannot stand." He was alone against them all.

She longed to enter, to take Him away with her, to show Him that her heart at least was faithful, to strain Him to her breast if He would allow her. "His Mother and His brethren came. And standing without sent unto Him, calling Him. And the multitude sat about Him. And they say to Him: Behold thy mother and thy brethren without seek for thee."

It was a moving moment, but Jesus was not moved. He had been bearing the harshness of His enemies; yet the moment He meets tenderness, the moment He becomes for His Mother an object of compassion, in that moment His seems to grow harsh Himself. It almost seemed that He scarcely deigned to notice that poor maternal love that was offered to Him, that frail refuge that she would have made for Him. "And answering them, He said: Who is my mother and my brethren?" In that place these words seem hard, even cruel. What is the mystery contained within them?

What that mystery is, He proceeds to show: "And looking round about on them who sat about Him, he saith: Behold my mother and my brethren. For whosoever shall do the will of God, he is my brother and my sister and my mother." Beyond the bonds of natural relationship appear the bonds of a new relationship, spiritual and outshining the first as the sun outshines the light of tapers. Natural relationship is not denied. The bonds that bind husband and wife, parents and children, master and servant, still remain. Indeed they are immeasurably ennobled (Eph. 5:21, 6:9). But above them are the bonds that bind the children of the Kingdom in a mysterious, more intimate kinship; and these are more precious and more profoundly interior to us, are beyond the power of time and relate us to each other by what is closest in us to God. Because this is so, the bonds of natural relationship become illicit and must be trampled under foot whenever they so act upon us as to weaken the spiritual relationship: "If any man come to me, and hate not his father and mother and wife and children and brethren and sisters, yea, and his own life also, he cannot be my disciple" (Luke 14:26). The saints are in no delusion as to what our Lord means, as we shall see.

Can it then have been that our Lord's kinsfolk had come to Capharnaum to dissuade Him from preaching—that, under the impulse of too earthly an affection, they were trying to deflect Him from the mission, entrusted Him by His father in heaven, of founding the Kingdom? It may be that His brethren were thus uncomprehending. But not His Mother. She knew too well that such a Son must be about His Father's business. She had come only to share the ignoring of sarcasm and blasphemy, and to be with Him visibly when the attack was visibly massing against Him. Why then the harshness of His word? Why should He thus refuse the gesture of her love?

It was of necessity that something in itself lawful, something incomparably pure and holy and delicate should be thus eternally broken. The Virgin's sacrifice could never be the renunciation of sin, for she had no sin; it could only be the renunciation of things holy for the sake of things holier. A physical tenderness that was holy had to be denied in order that men might know how they must treat physical tenderness that was not holy. It was of necessity that what was sinless in the Virgin should bear affliction and that the rightful desire of her heart to bring visible consolation to her Son should be cast aside in order that she might perfectly resemble her Son and that she might suffer in the likeness of Him who was to suffer and die in desolation. Thus, like to her Son and better than any who should come after her, she was to do "the will of God"; more fully than any who should come after her, she was to be to her Son a brother and a sister and a mother; more fully than any who should come after her, she was to enter into the Kingdom of God, the Kingdom of spiritual relationships. And of that Kingdom she was to be the Queen. The word of Jesus that called upon her to sacrifice the natural manifestation of her love was harsh only to the ear. Even more powerfully than the harsh words he was later to address to the Canaanite woman, His word to His mother wrought in her soul those mighty increases of divine charity by which she could consent to renunciations ever more total.

From that time the Virgin never again came to offer her Son consolation against insult or martyrdom. She remained afar off. She knew that such a loneliness He needed for the world's redemption. She troubled Him no more. Later, when He told them that He was the Son of the

Blessed God, He was once more treated by the Jews as a blasphemer and condemned to death (Mark 15:61–64). Once more—this time by Pilate's soldiers—he was thought to be mad. They stripped him and put a scarlet cloak about him; platting a crown of thorns they put it upon His head and a reed in His right hand; and bowing the knee before Him, they mocked Him saying Hail, King of the Jews (Matt. 26:28–29). But the Mother of Jesus made no move to draw near Him. She knew the bitter forms that the sorrow of separation must assume.

The gospel of St. Luke contains, in the parallel passage, the same teaching (Luke 11:17–28). St. Luke likewise gives us the reply that Jesus made when He was accused of casting out devils by Beelzebub "If Satan also be divided against himself, how shall his Kingdom stand?" St. Luke gives us further the parable of the unclean spirit which, being cast out of a man, walked through places without water, seeking rest and not finding takes with him seven other spirits more wicked than himself and returns to the place whence he came out so that the last state of that man is worse than the first. The unclean spirit is Satan who, formerly cast out of the house of Israel and finding it occupied by Christ, essays to return and bring the Jews down to a level lower than the pagans. The Jews understood the parable. Their hatred grew with their understanding. They became menacing.

It was then that a woman lifted up her voice in behalf of Jesus. It has been observed that women are bolder in taking the part of those who are insulted, their heart urges them and they speak out what they feel. There is an example of this in the life of St. Benedict Joseph Labre. One day in Rome he was attacked by eight or ten men who struck him, kicked him, flung him to the ground, spat upon him. A woman who was passing by, alone as she was, came to his rescue with an extraordinary air of authority; and as they sought to excuse themselves on the ground that he was mad and might therefore be mocked, she answered, "It is you who are mad, and he is a saint." That word on behalf of the saint of poverty was the direct echo, across the space of the years, of another voice which seventeen centuries earlier had been uplifted in Galilee to defend the King of poverty against His enemies. "As he spoke these things," says the gospel, "a certain woman from the crowd, lifting up her voice, said to him: Blessed is the womb that bore thee and the paps that gave thee suck." How enviable was the lot of that woman, to whom it was given to defend Jesus. Surely He, in His turn, would one day proclaim her Blessed.

Here the mystery is again upon us. If the woman had simply defended Jesus, perhaps he would have publicly praised and glorified her. But she had spoken of the Mother of Jesus. She had envied her who had had the glory of cradling Him and loving Him with the love that mothers have for their sons. And upon this point Jesus would tolerate no misunderstanding. Those who range themselves with His Mother merit to be treated by Him in some sense as He treated His Mother. They merit the realization that the sacrifice of the purest maternal tenderness has been demanded, and offered, for the foundation of the nobler Kingdom of spiritual relationships. They merit to be associated with some part of the mystery of separation.

Such an honour was accorded this woman great of heart, whose name is unknown and whose memory lives for ever. She had glorified Mary. But had she realized what Mary was? Had she realized that Mary's true glory was not to be the Mother of Jesus but to be a Mother worthy of Jesus? Had she realized that motherhood according to the flesh was for Mary but the sacrament of an ineffable grace whereby she was made to participate—in a manner altogether unique—in the communicable sanctity of the Saviour, which is the very foundation of the Kingdom of spiritual relations? Did she realize that the pain of visible separation from her Son, a pain that grew every moment, was demanded of her in order that she might be the first member of the new spiritual family, that she might be Mother according to grace of all men? How could she have realized all this or any of it?

So that Jesus proceeded to illumine her heart and unbare to her the most hidden glories of Mary. He corrected her faith, by giving it a new direction towards the great Kingdom of those who hear the word of God and keep it, of whom Mary is Queen—for she had, from the first day, kept and pondered in her heart the message that the Angel had announced to the shepherds (Luke 2:19), and the words the Child Himself had said at Jerusalem (Luke 2:51). All this is in our Lord's answer to the nameless woman: "Yea, rather blessed are they who hear the word of God and keep it" (Luke 11:28). "Yea, rather." It is as though Jesus made no comment upon what she had said to the praise of Mary. He did not deny it. But He would not leave it simply at that, she must go beyond it. He took hold of the faith that was coming to life in her and turned it firmly towards those spiritual realities which she barely glimpsed and of which the natural privileges of Mary were but the outward sacrament.

Yet how magnificent these privileges become once we grasp that they are the efficacious sign, the instrument, of the highest graces. Our Lady's motherhood according to the flesh, with all the agony and renunciation it demanded, becomes immeasurably more splendid when we know it as the cause of the purest love ever granted to a creature. Completed by Jesus' answer, the words of the great-hearted woman of Galilee begin to reveal the fullness of their meaning. Thus the Church can repeat them. In the mass *Salve sancta Parens* (of which the gospel is taken from this same passage of St. Luke) she joins them to those of Our Lord. She repeats them at the Communion, when Christ enters into us to communicate to us sacramentally a little of that love which on the day of the Incarnation he communicated to the Virgin in such abundance: "Blessed is the womb of the Virgin Mary which bore the Son of the eternal Father!" By setting down here, in a more perfect light, the acclamation of the unknown woman, the Church continues to fulfill through the ages the Virgin's prophecy: "Behold, from henceforth all generations shall call me blessed."

A sword should pierce her soul and all generations should call her blessed—blessed because in the likeness of her Son, she bore suffering and desolation in their fullness.

Is the interpretation we have given of the passages of scripture concerning the Blessed Virgin necessarily the true one? Is it certain that Jesus, under the external semblance of repulsing His Mother's tenderness, was actually binding her to Him still closer by an interior love and associating her with Himself in the work of redemption? An episode which took place at the beginning of His public life but which we have held in reserve till now, seems to put the matter beyond question. It is the episode at Cana (John 2:1–11).

There was a marriage in Cana of Galilee, and the mother of Jesus was there. And the wine failing, those who were giving the feast were ashamed. Jesus' mother saw this and said to her son: "They have no wine." Verbally, this was a mere statement of fact. Actually she was asking for a miracle. Then came our Lord's mysterious answer: "Woman, what is it to me and to thee? My hour is not yet come." The literal translation is as we have given it—What is it to me and to thee? The bearing of this phrase, used to this day by the Arabs in Palestine, is roughly expressed by the words "Leave it to me." The whole meaning depends upon the tone in which the phrase is uttered—it might signify impatience or rebuke or indifference. In the present instance, all three of these possible implications are negatived by the event. But they can also bear within them great tenderness, signifying: "Do not be disturbed, I have seen all, all is well, leave it to me." And it was thus that Jesus spoke to His Mother.

He called her Woman, as at the hour when He was nailed to the cross (John 19:26), a word of reverence—for He was speaking to her as God, in regard to a solemn matter, one that went beyond the framework of family relations, for it touched upon the destiny of the Kingdom of God.

It reads as though Jesus was quite clearly refusing the implied but unspoken request of His Mother. He did it with great gentleness and He gave her His reason—that the hour for the inauguration of His public life of preaching and miracles was not yet come. The meaning seems perfectly clear: Mary must trust in Him without reserve, must leave the whole matter entirely in His hands: and so, indeed, she had done from the beginning.

But here what seemed so clear is suddenly cast into darker mystery. Jesus had just told His Mother that His hour was not yet come, and she acted as if He had said the reverse. She seemed to take the miracle for granted. "His mother said to the waiters: Whatsoever he shall say to you, do ye."

Here is the key to the mystery. If there had not been the prayer of Mary, the hour fixed from all eternity for the inauguration of Jesus' public ministry would have come later, and Jesus, who was to accredit the message He bore to men by signs and wonders, would have awaited some other occasion to manifest Himself—would have made a paralytic walk, or given sight to a blind man, or cleansed a leper. This is what Jesus

Himself was affirming when He told His Mother that in this sense His hour was not yet come. But at the same moment, by a secret illumination with which He filled her heart, He willed her to know that from all eternity the hour of His public ministry had been advanced because of the humble prayer she had just uttered. There is profound tenderness, an infinite delicacy of love half-hidden under the mystery, restraint and even, as some readers feel, coldness of the words recorded by St. John. Marvellous, too, the power of the Virgin's prayer. A thought of her heart, a word uttered by her with the desire to relieve the mildest of human embarrassments—the thought and the word were foreknown from all eternity, and from all eternity the hour was set forward at which Jesus should begin the public preaching of the Kingdom of God. Nothing so great has ever been said, or ever will be said, upon the might of her intercession as the gospel story of the miracle of Cana. It was the hour of Mary's power.

The Virgin had all power over the heart of her Son. She had done His will too utterly for Him to refuse to do hers—*Voluntatem timentium se faciet* (Psalm 144:19)—the Lord will do the will of them that fear him with the loving fear of a child for its father. And in fact Jesus speaks: "Fill the water-pots with water, And they filled them to the brim. And he said to them: Draw out now, and carry to the chief steward of the feast.... This beginning of miracles did Jesus in Cana of Galilee and manifested his glory. And his disciples believed in him." It was to the intervention of the Virgin that they owed their belief in Him thus early.

Mary was close to her Son in the bond of love. But at the same time, the suffering of separation, which had lain in her heart from the day the Child had slipped away from her in Jerusalem, began to grow and did not cease its growing from the moment when His public life opened. That suffering held supreme tests in store for her.

ce ce ce ce ce ce ce ce ce ce ce ce ce ce ce ce ce ce ce ce ce ce ce ce ce

THE LAST FOUR SORROWS

The external separation of the Mother from her Son grew greater as the Passion proceeded.

FOURTH SORROW

This was Mary's sufferings while Jesus was making the way of the cross. Pilate had delivered Jesus to the Jews. The Roman soldiers had taken Him to crucify Him. The custom was to make the condemned man carry his own cross. No exception was made for Jesus: "And they took Jesus and led him forth. And bearing his own cross, he went forth to that place which is called the place of the skull, in Hebrew Golgotha" (John 19:16–17). But they soon saw that Jesus was too weak and that he might die under the load. When, according to the Synoptic gospels, they were outside the town, "they laid hold of one Simon of Cyrene, coming from the country, and they laid the cross on him to carry after Jesus" (Luke 23:26). After that Jesus did not carry his cross. He walked before the others on the road to Calvary. And, says St. Luke, "there followed him a great multitude of people, and of women, who bewailed and lamented him. But Jesus turning to them said: Daughters of Jerusalem, weep not over me; but weep for yourselves and for your children" (Luke 23:27–28). Let us pause at the fourth sorrow.

Beyond the rabble of men and women, there to mock at Jesus, drawn to where He was by hatred and evil instinct, there were a handful of women, some of whom doubtless had known and loved Him, their hearts filled with pity. Among them was the Virgin. She made no effort, as once at Capharnaum, to draw near her Son to protect Him. Her natural love was by now utterly broken and offered up. It was not for her to approach Jesus with consolation. She of all people must respect the lonely dereliction in which the world's salvation must be wrought. She wept, then, hidden among the women. And when Jesus stopped to speak, she knew from the beginning that for her He would have no word. It was to the women of Jerusalem that He spoke. He did not wish that they should weep for Him. He wished for no natural consolation. Let them weep for themselves and for their children. But the Virgin, who wept in the midst of them—for her Child she had no need to weep. She must weep for other women's children, for the children of those who were bringing her Son to His death. She had accepted fully, totally. But she must be broken anew, her nature more utterly crushed.

At that moment her task took on a new sublimity. She wept for the sins of men, she suffered not for herself but for the world's salvation. Her suffering, bound close to His, was a co-redemptive suffering. She learnt what new regions of suffering love must seek out for itself if men were to be snatched from the terrible rigours of suffering that lay in wait for them. What these rigours were Jesus lets us glimpse in one lightning flash of revelation. To reveal the significance of the Passion, He draws aside for an instant the veils of the present and, in a phrase which is a supreme admonition of His love, lays bare before us the measureless demands of divine Justice. "For behold the days shall come, wherein they will say: Blessed are the barren and the wombs that have not borne and the paps that have not given suck. Then shall they begin to say to the mountains: Fall upon us. And to the hills: Cover us. For if in the green wood they do these things, what shall be done in the dry" (Luke 23:29–31). If divine justice requires such suffering of the innocent, what does it hold in store for the guilty? If to make its fire it will take the green wood, how shall it spare the dry?

At that time the Virgin Mary knew the mysterious immensity of the Redemption. On the one hand she saw all the extent of the world's sins and on the other the intensity and the infinite value of the sorrow at whose cost they were atoned. In the steps of her Son, she descended still further, with all her being, into the depths of the redemptive suffering.

FIFTH SORROW

Death was to break the last of the natural links still remaining mysteriously to bind the Virgin and her Son. "And when they were come to the place which is called Calvary, they crucified him there" (Luke 23:33). "Now there stood by the cross of Jesus, his mother and his mother's sister, Mary of Cleophas, and Mary Magdalen" (John 19:25). Mary was at the foot of the cross whereon her Son was crucified. This was the fifth of her sorrows.

Mary stood at the foot of the cross. She showed no weakening. She was not upheld by the holy women. On the contrary, in that moment she was upholding the whole Church by the irresistible upward movement of her love, strong as death. Standing erect she heard the Seven Last Words that came down from the height of the Cross into the desolation of her heart. *Stabat Mater dolorosa.*

Mary was close to the cross. But she made no move to embrace it. She remained a little away. In that last hour above all she must remain, in spite of her love, separated from her Son. When He cried out, "I thirst," it was not she, but the soldiers who, putting a sponge full of vinegar about hyssop, put it to his mouth (John 19:28–29).

It might seem that she had now given all, that there was no more to be stripped from her. But Jesus required of her one last separation more agonizing than all. To lose her Son, she must not wait till He was dead. While He still lived He must break once for all the last bond of that purest of natural love that He felt rising toward Him from the foot of the cross. It was His will to die poor, without even a mother. From now she must accept that another should be the object of her maternal tenderness. "When Jesus therefore had seen his mother and the disciple standing whom he loved, he said to his mother: Woman, behold thy son" (John 19:26).

For John the words were a joy unspeakable. But to Mary they were shattering. Of course she loved the disciple Jesus loved. But what an exchange. "For Jesus," cried St. Bernard, "she was given John; for the Lord, the servant; for the Master, the disciple; for the Son of God the son of Zebedee; for the true God, a mere man." In the same sermon St. Bernard tells us: "It was sharper than a sword, it pierced her very soul, unto the division of soul and spirit.... Be not amazed, my brethren, if it be said that Mary knew martyrdom in her heart."

Yet she remained erect at the foot of the cross. She was still there when the soldiers, having broken the legs of the two thieves, came to Jesus: "When they saw that he was already dead, they did not break his legs. But one of the soldiers with a spear opened his side, and immediately there came out blood and water" (John 19:33–34). At that moment the suffering of the Saviour was at an end, the world's Redemption was accomplished. But the co-redemptive suffering was not ended; it must go on till the day when, under the pressure of a love that grew without ceasing, body and soul came to the separation of death. In the deepest depths of her soul, Mary felt the thrust of the lance. It was the crowning agony of the fifth sorrow.

SIXTH SORROW

"And when it was evening, there came a certain rich man of Arimathea, named Joseph, who also himself was a disciple of Jesus. He went to Pilate and asked the body of Jesus. Then Pilate commanded that the body should be delivered" (Matt. 27:57–8). St. Luke (23:53) and St. John (19:38) give us the detail that Joseph of Arimathea himself took down the body of Jesus from the cross. There is no doubt that the holy women helped him in this, nor that Mary received her Son's body at the foot of the cross. Thus the Liturgy tells further that when the body of Jesus was brought down from the cross, His Mother received Him in her arms and held Him close to her; and it compared her with the Sunamitess (4 Kings 4:20) who when the child miraculously announced to her by the prophet was dead had held it upon her knees. Thus soberly, in three or four words, the Liturgy calls up the image of the Pietà which has so powerfully moved the souls of Christian people.

At last the Mother could embrace her Son. All the lovely memories of His childhood were in the embrace, but alas only to sharpen the pain. She could hold Him to her because He was beyond the reach of consolation. All alone, without aid from any human creature, He had drunk the chalice of His Passion and Death. In her arms she held with measureless reverence that sacred body which, though separated from His soul, yet remained immediately united to the very Person of the Word. She saw the wounds, but it was too late to heal them. "From the sole of the foot unto the top of the head, there is no soundness therein: wounds and bruises and swelling sores" (Is. 1:6). And even this poor contact was only for a short space.

SEVENTH SORROW

Yet there was no movement of rebellion in her, no violence of outcry against those who came to take her Son's body and place it in the tomb.

Joseph of Arimathea had brought fine linen to wrap His body (Mark 15:46). Nicodemus was with him. "They took therefore the body of Jesus and bound it in linen cloths, with the spices, as the manner of the Jews is to bury. Now there was in the place where he was crucified a garden: and in the garden a new sepulchre, wherein no man yet had been laid. There, therefore, because of the Parasceve of the Jews, they laid Jesus because the sepulchre was nigh at hand" (John 19:40–42). It was a new sorrow for the Virgin to have to leave her Son. But there was no weakening in her.

From now a new life began for her. Her role henceforth was to be at the heart of the church militant, sustaining it by the silence of her contemplation and her love. Action was for others. The gospel speaks of Mary Magdalen and the other Mary who, after Joseph of Arimathea had gone, remained a space sitting near the tomb (Matt. 27:60–61), while the other women went off to prepare spices and ointments (Luke 23:56), for the embalming of Jesus could not be long delayed. We hear of them again on the morning of Easter Sunday, and we hear of John to whom the Virgin had been given as Mother, and of others beside. But of the Virgin herself, no word. All her life was within. Long ago she had heard the first words of Jesus and had kept them in her heart. And now she had heard His last words, the Seven Last Words, the least of which would have given her matter for meditation for all the time still remaining to her upon earth.

She knew that the work of Christ in Himself was consummated, and that the work of Christ in the totality of His members, the Church, had begun. She had not preached; she had contemplated, loved, suffered during the public life of Jesus. And now that He had founded the church in His blood, her part was still not to preach but to contemplate, love, suffer. Scripture mentioned her once more—before Pentecost—but only to show her prayer mingled with that of the apostles, the brethren of Jesus and the Christian community: "All these were persevering with one mind in prayer, with the women and Mary the mother of Jesus, and with his brethren" (Acts 1:14). On the evening of His burial, when Joseph of Arimathea had gone and the lights of the Sabbath had begun to shine in Jerusalem, she knew of her own knowledge that from now on she had no one here below upon whom she could lean, she knew what a weight of suffering Jesus had laid upon her in making her our Mother. It was the seventh of her sorrows.

O all you who come into this world to suffer, "behold and see if there be any sorrow like unto my sorrow." And you, my brother, for whom she has wept, over whom she had wept, "do not forget, in the depth of your heart, the weeping of your Mother, that the propitiation and benediction of those days may be accomplished in you."

"THY own soul a sword shall pierce." From the first sorrow to the seventh, the sword of Simeon's prediction had cut steadily deeper into her heart, bringing her the realized knowledge of ever-new suffering. Now at the end she was more desolate even than the Jerusalem of the prophet's lamentation: "To what shall I compare thee, or to what shall I liken thee, O Daughter of Jerusalem? To what shall I equal thee, that I may comfort thee, O Virgin daughter of Sion? For great as the sea is thy destruction" (Lam. 2:13). But she remained strong in sorrow. Neither her soul nor her frail body knew an instant's wavering. If in the strict sense she did not actually undergo martyrdom, her love and courage immeasurably surpassed the love and courage of the martyrs. And her suffering likewise exceeded theirs; she bore more than they of the terrible burden of the world's sin. She was a martyr eminently, as the philosophers say, if not formally. She surpasses all virgins in purity and all martyrs in fortitude; so that the Liturgy can hail her in the last responsory of Matins as first rose of martyrs, lily among virgins:

Ave princeps generosa,
Martyrumque prima rosa,
Virginumque lilium.

And at the Communion of the Mass of the Seven Dolors: "Happy the senses of the Blessed Virgin Mary which, without dying, earned the palm of martyrdom beneath the cross of our Lord."

208

Who then, so well as the Virgin of Compassion, can reveal to us the depths of the mystery of the Passion? If only we too before death might have some small fragment of her knowledge of that mystery. At least we can long for it and pray with the church: "O God, at whose passion, as Simeon foretold, the most sweet soul of Mary thy glorious Virgin Mother was pierced by a sword of sorrow, mercifully grant that we who reverently meditate upon her sorrows may reap the happy fruit of thy Passion."

St. John of the Cross speaks, in the *Living Flame of Love*, of the transfixion of the heart as a marvellous grace, granted to the small number of souls which have been faithful to love to the end and above all to those whose love and whose spirit are to be carried forward through the ages in a succession of sons; for, says the Mystical Doctor, God deposits in the founders a richness of spiritual power capable of vivifying all the long line of their followers. It is as though their hearts must be pierced in order that the flood of grace may pour out for the enrichment of the rest.

Tire transfixion of the Virgin's heart is a mystery of love and suffering still higher and more radiant than the prodigious transfixion granted to St. Francis and St. Teresa. Erect at the foot of the Cross, the Virgin received, in that heart which was opening to the whole world, a spiritual love so strong and flaming and tender and universal that it could reach out to embrace every single one of those whom her Son had given to be her sons to the end of the earth and the end of time. Thus the transfixion of the Virgin's heart approached nearer than any other the Transfixion of the Heart of Jesus, the sole source of the world's redemption.

HILAIRE BELLOC

ↄ ↄ

OUR LORD AND OUR LADY

They warned Our Lady for the Child
　　That was Our blessed Lord,
And She took Him into the desert wild,
　　Over the camel's ford.

And a long song She sang to Him
　　And a short story told:
And She wrapped Him in a woollen cloak
　　To keep Him from the cold.

But when Our Lord was grown a man
　　The Rich they dragged Him down,
And they crucified Him in Golgotha,
　　Out and beyond the Town.

They crucified Him on Calvary,
　　Upon an April day;

And because He had been her little Son
She followed Him all the way.

Our Lady stood beside the Cross,
A little space apart,
And when She heard Our Lord cry out
A sword went through Her Heart.

They laid Our Lord in a marble tomb,
Dead, in a winding sheet.
But Our Lady stands above the world
With the white Moon at her Feet.

MAURICE ZUNDEL

ℐ ℐ

OUR LADY OF CALVARY

St. John of the Cross and St. Teresa have expressed, precisely and magnificently, the normal development of mystical experience.[1]

They have told of the terrible intensity of that light which exiles the creature from himself by cutting him off from his sense-activity, his intellect, even from God as He had till then been known.

They have described the suspension over the abyss, the utter isolation, the burning sense of unworthiness, the inexorable dark, the reduction to nothingness whose horror is past all saying and which seems to dislocate the soul in a fearful anathema. They have told of the ecstasies that seem to ravish the soul from the body, the sudden illuminations which bathe it in infinite light, the joy so violent that it must bring death if God did not intervene to prevent that effect.

This initiation is not of course accompanied, in all souls that abandon themselves to the divine embrace, by all the phenomena and all the favours described in *The Interior Castle*. Many experience none of these mysterious visitations save the wholly interior action which preserves

---

1.   See *Three Mystics*, ed. Fr. Bruno, O.D.C.

the secret of them, and thus do not clearly discern the stages they pass through in an obscurity which hides them from themselves. But the one thing rigorously necessary for all souls is that they should die to the spirit of possession that rivets them to self and become, in the spirit of poverty, wholly God's.

When the gift is consummated and the whole being utterly receptive to the divine mode of the transforming union, the body is so perfectly interior to the soul and the soul so perfectly interior to God, that contemplation is no longer the faintest difficulty. On the contrary, contemplation not only stirs to life in each an echo of itself, but also it finds in each the cooperation of a new urge. All the fibres of the being are but one voice hymning God. Creatures are no longer an obstacle: they enter the marvellous cycle in which their night sparkles like a procession of stars in a summer sky. They are no longer external but within us, all loved, all as brethren, each regaining its fullness of reality in the ray of ineffable love with which God loves it.

It is perfect joy in divine freedom, and the Canticle of the Sun is its eternal music.

THE soul of course still remains capable of suffering, not now for itself, but as a victim of love for the salvation of others.

It is by this title alone that the Mother of the Creator knew the trials of the interior life. She had no need to be purified, for nothing in her opposed the least resistance to the accomplishment of the kingdom of God. She was "above the weakness of ecstasy," for in ecstasy is manifested the rigidity of a nature in which all is not wholly obedient to the movement of the Spirit.

All her suffering was for others, and as she was offered from the first instant of her existence, the Liturgy of blood that was to be consummated on Calvary began for her at her conception.

It is not within our power to follow all the development or trace all the upward movements of her love.

Think for a moment of the anguish of Joan of Arc at the pity of the realm of France, or the agony of Catherine of Siena at the wounds of the Church: and you will have some faint conception of the burning solicitude in the heart of the Virgin.

If you have ever seen a nun bending over the bed of a dying man left by his own to his misery, and uttering the words which give him back his childhood, you will have a figure of the maid of Nazareth, bending over a world in agony with all the tenderness of a charity which suffers immeasurably more from its compassion than the sufferer from his disease: for she knows what is the disease with which all are ill and who must be the Victim for all their wounds.

> *Despised and the most abject of men,*
> *A man of sorrows and acquainted with infirmity;*
> *And his look was as it were hidden and despised,*
> > *Whereupon we esteemed him not.*
> *Surely he hath borne our infirmities*
> > *And carried our sorrows;*
> *And we have thought of him as it were a leper,*
> > *And as one struck by God and afflicted.*
> > *But he was wounded for our iniquities.*
> > *He was bruised for our sins;*
> *The chastisement of our peace was upon him*
> *And by his bruises we are healed.* (Is. 53:3–5)

She could not read the words without being overwhelmed by distress, recognising in opprobrium the secret of His life, though she did not yet know that it would be as His mother that she would see the torment of the Man of Sorrows upon whom "Yahweh has caused to fall all our iniquity."

When she stood at the foot of the Cross, she saw all the instants of her life converging towards this unique moment in which she must take into herself the death agony of God.

The synoptic gospels tell us, with an objectivity equal to their reserve, the state of abandonment to which the soul of Jesus was delivered "When his hour was come." They make us see that His death was a torment inflicted by no human hand and that it gained His body only after crucifying His soul.

Comment would be as futile as sacrilegious. St. Paul has said the one word which would cast light upon those depths: "He was made sin for us."[2]

There is the ineffable centre of the mystery. Jesus *felt* himself identified with Evil—whose horror He knew in the vision of God—felt himself as made to bear the responsibility for all man's denials of God, felt their appalling reality so laid upon Him that his very executioners may have seemed to have less guilt than He was bearing in the infinite anathema that was crushing Him down.[3]

---

2. Cf. 2 Cor. 5:21. What it says is: "Him that knew no sin, for us he hath made sin, that we might be made the justice of God in Him."

3. Cf. Fr. Vincent McNabb, O.P., *From a Friar's Cell,* pp. 176, 191. This true theologian shows with admirable penetration the obscurity to which the *acquired* knowledge of Jesus might be subjected, and the suffering of which it might be the source. I have never read anything which shed so much light on an episode that one cannot think of save in trembling.

All the beatific brightness shining at the summit of His spirit, all the holiness of His love, could but render more torturing this death-clutch of the darkness which held His soul so inexorably.

The evening before, His bodily senses had uttered all their distress in the sweat of blood, and now He breathes forth His soul in the cry which beat upon Mary's heart with the shattering force of a divine catastrophe:

My God, my God, why hast Thou forsaken Me? (Matt. 15:34)

What part had she in His darkness?

It would be rash to make any affirmation whatsoever. Yet we may at least remind ourselves that Mary lived by faith and not in the face to face vision of God.

She believed, she did not see.

She had, we may be sure, received the most certain assurances of the mystery which had been accomplished within her. Yet its reality was for her not an object of knowledge but of faith.

May it have been by the fissure which lies between faith and sight that she was invaded by the darkness which submerged the soul of her Son? If so, she did not cease to adhere with unshakable certainty to the Word which had always been her guide.

Yet it seems that if such a trial were reserved for her, as is probable, it was not at this moment.

Her share had still, it would appear, an exclusively maternal character. As other women bring to the dying the luminous gift of supreme tenderness, she brought a mother's heart to the death agony of God. And she alone realised the immensity of the tragedy which centered all human history in the crucifixion of Love.

God died and He was her Son:

And she was His mother.

The one being who could be with Him, she stood erect in her inviolable solitude, offering her innocence as witness of His, making all his opprobrium wholly her own, stricken with all our denials, suffering the pain of all His wounds.

He looked upon her. He saw her sorrowing in all His sorrows, pierced through with His distress, bearing in all her being the wound of Love pitilessly condemned. In a creation rebellious from its beginning, she at least was wholly His.

And He gave her to us: *Behold thy Mother.*

In this He really made her His mother in each of us: *Mater pulchrae dilectionis*: Mother of Beautiful Love; but in what an abyss of sorrow she received the title.

For her we are ever the children of the *Stabat.* She is bound to us with the same love which binds her to Him. So she stands as long as the divine agony endures.[4] She hastens to us to take Him down from the Cross of whose torment our egoism is the daily, hourly, renewal.

It is so that she sees all, in that terrible greatness in which each one of us appears as responsible for her Son, responsible for the blood that was shed, responsible for the reign of love whose price He was.

It is so that she loves us in the eternal wisdom in which man takes on his true face, in the light of that sacred Face whose ineffable mystery she presents to us: as the light of the candle in which the whole world lives anew.

---

4   Jesus will be in agony till the end of the world, we must not sleep the while" (Pascal).

Lumen Christi
Deo gratias!
Light of Christ,
Thanks be to God.

CHARLES JOURNET

⊄ ⊄

"THE SWOON"

A petition having been addressed to Pope Julius II asking him to authorize and indulgence the feast *De spasmo Beatae Virginis Mariae*—the French title was Notre-Dame de la Pàmoison (our Lady of the Swoon)—which was being celebrated with an octave from Passion Sunday to Palm Sunday, the pope charged Cardinal Cajetan to examine the question whether such a feast could be accepted as canonical.

We have Cajetan's reply, written at Rome and dated July 17th, 1506. Let it be said to the great theologian's glory, that if he was to be in error, some years later, in holding it as more probable that the Virgin was conceived with original sin, he deserved well of her in this present matter and showed the love he had vowed her.

He was against the idea of Our Lady swooning. First, because St. John describes her as "standing" at the foot of the Cross. Then, because the Virgin like her Son could bear suffering without wavering. If it is true that she is full of grace, we must deny all the corporeal infirmities which are an obstacle to the plenitude and perfection of grace. If the Virgin had swooned, she would have been unable to remain constantly united to her Son by the loving grieving contemplation of the Passion.

This sorrowful contemplation was the highest and holiest form that her compassion could take. After the suffering of Christ, that of His Mother was unquestionably the most intense that has ever been; but it did not diminish the full domination of the soul over the body and the feelings.

Cajetan concludes, therefore, while submitting his decisions to the judgment of the Holy See, that if it was desired to celebrate a feast of the Sorrows of Mary, this feast should not be called her "Swoon." Another name should be chosen and another place assigned it in the liturgical calendar. The teaching Church has confirmed his judgment—completely as to the first point since it does not invoke Our Lady of the Swoon; and partially as to the second, since it limits the first feast of the Seven Sorrows to the Friday after Passion Sunday.

In his work *De festis Domini Nostri Jesu Christi, Beatae Mariae Virginis et quorumdam Sanctorum*, Benedict XIV, discussing this first feast of the Seven Sorrows, cites with approval Cajetan's treatment of the Swoon and criticizes the painters and preachers who make Our Lady's sorrows too much like those of women in general or who represent her as sunk deep in despair. He reminds us of the great phrase of St. Ambrose about Our Lady: "She was not ignorant of the mystery that she had given birth to a child who was to rise from the dead."

What St. Thomas Aquinas says, commenting on St. Basil, remains the last word: That while she was at the foot of the Cross and remembered past glories—Gabriel's message, the ineffable revelation of the divine conception, the great series of miracles—the Blessed Virgin felt her soul "fluctuate," for on the one hand she saw her Son in the depths of abjection, and on the other she remembered his triumphs.

LIMBO

The ancient greyness shifted
Suddenly and thinned
Like mist upon the moors
Before a wind.
An old, old prophet lifted
A shining face and said:
"He will be coming soon.
The Son of God is dead;
He died this afternoon."

A murmurous excitement stirred
All souls.
They wondered if they dreamed—
Save one old man who seemed
Not even to have heard.

And Moses standing,
Hushed them all to ask

If any had a welcome song prepared.
If not, would David take the task?
And if they cared
Could not the three young children sing
The Benedicite, the canticle of praise
They made when God kept them from perishing
In the fiery blaze?

A breath of spring surprised them,
Stilling Moses' words.
No one could speak, remembering
The first fresh flowers,
The little singing birds.
Still others thought of fields new ploughed
Or apple trees
All blossom-boughed.
Or some, the way a dried bed fills
With water
Laughing down green hills.
The fisherfolk dreamed of the foam
On bright blue seas.
The one old man who had not stirred
Remembered home.

And there He was
Splendid as the morning sun and fair
As only God is fair.
And they, confused with joy,

Knelt to adore
Seeing that He wore
Five crimson stars
He never had before.

No canticle at all was sung.
None toned a psalm, or raised a greeting song.
A silent man alone
Of all that throng
Found tongue—
Not any other.

Close to His heart
When the embrace was done,
Old Joseph said, "How is Your Mother,
How is Your Mother, Son?"

C. C. MARTINDALE, S.J.

ᘏ ᘏ

MOTHER OF THE MYSTICAL BODY

The direct meaning of Our Lord's two brief sentences—"Woman, behold thy son": "Behold thy mother"—was that He entrusted His Mother to His best-beloved disciple as a sacred charge. This fact, too, is not without significance. It is not as though He had Himself been able, for the last few years, to have charge of her. Throughout His ministry it had been with other relatives that she lived. They had been unsympathetic, and, after this catastrophe, would be even more so, at least till they had learnt to believe in the Resurrection. But John's understanding of Jesus was greater than theirs ever would become. And it was not going to be John's destiny to travel far, like St. Thomas or even St. Peter: he could exercise his charge continuously. And finally, we are to be shown that it was in the group of Apostles that Mary was, at least at first, to tarry: she was to be there, early on the day of Pentecost; and afterwards, accessible to the evangelists and St. Luke in particular.

To some it has seemed arbitrary to say more than that, or even so much. But, if we revert to the great principle of the Mystical Body of Christ and to our incorporation with Him, we see that we are driven to say much more! For in that Mystical Body, Mary too exists. And within it, she holds a position that is not ours and cannot be. She is the Mother of *Christ*. Therefore she is Mother of the *whole* Christ, in whom are we, incorporate. You cannot as it were detach and departmentalise Mary, and make her exclusively Mother of Christ in so far as He lived at Nazareth or sojourned in Palestine. She is, altogether and always, what at any time and in any way she was. Our Lord's words on the Cross to her and to the disciple are, then, in the last resort, rather a declaration of what God's plan about the Incarnation and the Church which is its prolongation, involved, than the inauguration of a new relationship.

CAUSE OF OUR JOY

O mother of fair love, it was not alone
Christ whom you mothered on the first Christinas night,
not alone the Orient, the Splendor that outshone
daylight and suns and all created light.
It was not only this new dearness, kissed and held
in love and lullabies among the straw,
warmed by the breath of oxen that still smelled
of clover and sweet fields. But in deep awe
there crept in with the shepherd and his sheep
and bowed down with the Oriental king
your other children who will always keep
the joy of your mysterious mothering,
cause of our joy, heaven's gate, at once our mother,
on that first Christmas night, through Christ, our Brother.

ᴄᴈ ᴄᴈ

THE ASSUMPTION

Of Our Lady it has often been said that she was the only one among our purely human race with whom God has had altogether His own way. True, it was, mysteriously, His way that she should suffer great sorrow, and die the death that we do, yet who can wonder, since that was His way even with His Divine Son, who was also hers. We are not lingering over that, nor over the theology of our Redemption through pain and death. Enough to say that she herself would have suffered yet more, had she not been allowed to go along with her divine Son also in His anguish. But what we are insisting upon is this, that God triumphed from the outset and continuously within her soul, and the Church forthwith felt her to be the beginning of a new world, a new race, a second Eve who should be more truly the Mother of all living than the first was, inasmuch as Mary's soul never took into itself spiritual death, nor was the "more abundant life" ever excluded from it.

It is, in reality, in terms of this conviction that the Church began to see her as immaculate, undeprived of that Original Grace of which we are deprived—in a word, and more positively, "graced" from the first moment of her existence as God would have wished us all to be. With us, speaking reverently, He has not had His way in that matter: Adam cast from him, by his sin, the supernatural life, and could not in any way transmit to us that grace which he no more had. We are conceived, not with it, as God would have desired, but without it. But in this sense Mary was exempted from our disaster—the grace that we receive at Baptism, she received at the first moment of her existence. Of the Immaculate Conception something is said later. Here we wish to say that the general belief in Our Lady's Assumption is not indeed defined as a dogma, though it soon may be defined: in any event it is one that a Catholic would be *positively* rash to reject. It is itself, like the dogma of the Immaculate Conception, not an independent, separate belief, but is caught up into the covering truth that we began by stating—Mary never interposed any obstacle to the will and the grace of God—God had His own way with her from beginning to end.

From this it does not follow of absolute necessity that her soul should be already reunited with her body, but we can see that almost inevitably it does so follow. For it was not really the plan nor wish of God that human souls should exist in a disembodied state. We are, and are for ever destined to be, men and women, and by no means angels. It is, in a sense, a violent and unnatural condition, for a human soul to be discarnate. Philosophers, I think, have a hard task to settle what manner of knowledge and memory can then belong to it. In a word, we were not created to be angels, who are pure spirits never having had affinity with a body; but we, that is, our souls, are spirits so created as to "set towards" a body, in fact, each of them towards *that* body along with which it makes up a true person, body-soul. If then, indeed, God had His own way, from beginning to end, with Mary, and is having it now, it is difficult to see how He could allow her soul to endure discarnate.

It is worth noticing that in any case the event commemorated by the Feast of the Assumption is outside of human verification. The legends relating the gathering together of the Apostles at Jerusalem, the burial by them of Mary, and their discovery of her tomb empty after three days, cannot be proved to be historical, though they witness to a tradition in the Church and such traditions are never negligible. Traditions are not the product of the legend, but give rise to it. But even these legends contain no hint of apparitions of Our Lady in bodily form, after her death, comparable with those of Our Lord after His Resurrection, and indeed this instantly gives a much higher value to the tradition, because had it supplied the slightest chance to the legend to model itself further upon the Gospel stories, the legend would most certainly have done so. But the reuniting of Mary's soul with her body was an event that of necessity escaped all human observation; there was no need at all that her glorified body should have been seen by or even see-able to human eyes. It would seem nearer to the truth to say that the normal condition of a glorified body is a non-spatial one, to say that it somehow *can* become spatial, than to think of it as usually spatial. When Our Lord appeared to His Apostles and said: "A [mere] spirit hath not flesh and bones as ye see me having" (Luke 24:39), He was condescending, by exception, to their human needs. It comes back to this. We mean, by the Resurrection of the Body, that we shall not only be for ever men and women, but the same men and women. Our soul will so be controlling matter as to make one person with it—it is, in reality, the soul that catches up our material coefficient into a personal unity. But it is only too obvious that scientifically we have no idea what matter is. We do know that it is not spirit—that is about as far as we can go. Therefore we can see that a body-soul—let alone a glorified Body-Soul, need occupy no space at all. Yet again, we see that it *can*. Our Lord, who in His glorified self passed through the stone of the Tomb and the doors of the Upper Chamber, and at will ceased altogether to be visible, yet became at times "three-dimensional," was acting as He *could* act when it was desirable, for the Apostles' sake, that He should so act. But His words: "A [mere] spirit hath not flesh and bones as ye see me having," and His act of cooking the fish over a fire—the very last things that the Apostles would have invented if they did not really happen—dispose of the modernist idea that Christ rose because somehow the Apostles felt He was with them still and working powerfully in their souls. It is much better to say that the words were not spoken and that the event never occurred, than to volatilise the whole thing into a falsely mystical piece of impressionism.[1]

But what we want to reach is a point where, forgetting argument, we are enabled to rejoice in the plenitude of Our Lady's joy.

What I would first ask you to try to recall is the terrific energy latent or actually operative in the world. I do not mean to dwell on abstruse topics like the explosive forces latent in the atom, on the appalling rapidity of light, the speed of the rotation of our world, the tremendous tugs of gravitation, because after all in a sense those facts are relative. It is to us that they seem rapid, tremendous and so forth. I am not asking you, even, to reflect upon the stored-up energies of dynamite, or, in short, of anything that is not yourselves. But what I would ask you to observe is the tremendous reserve of force that exists in *yourselves*.

---

1.   That Our Lady should have appeared, for example, to the eyes of Bernadette at Lourdes, proves nothing at all about her body being glorified and reunited to her soul. Angels and (at present) Saints have often appeared to the "eyes" of men still upon earth; but they are pure spirits, and the impression upon the senses of the seer has to be explained along quite different lines.

The lightning-swift rapidity with which you blink if dazzled, or even if a fly flickers before your eye: the instant reaction of your arm if anyone seems suddenly on the verge of attacking you: the force with which you even habitually move, which is proved by the bruises that are made if you accidentally hit up against something hard, even *without noticing that you do so*! Even the astounding feats of energy that you can deploy if you are suddenly stimulated to do so. Thus I knew a youth who leapt a six-foot hawthorn hedge because a murder or a suicide (it was never quite proved which) was being enacted behind it, and it never occurred to him to do anything but try to stop it. So he jumped, and *could* jump. When the mess behind the hedge had been cleared up, he was left bewildered as how to get back across the hedge again, and had to go a long way round. Our life is compact of things that we do not do, because we think we can't: but we could, if we cared enough; and we would care enough if we saw clearly enough without distracting, neutralising visions.

Now, as things are, life is one mass of distractions. We see something, but we see so many other things at the same time that we cannot realise it. This is one reason for the inertia of clever people or politicians or, in fact, of all those who see too many things at the same time. Hence it becomes almost impossible to care about any one thing *sufficiently* to sacrifice everything else for it, as the man did for the One Perfect Pearl. This again is why Christians do not habitually care sufficiently about Christ to give up everything for Him. Still, there have been, in the lives of most, moments of vivid illumination when they were, as we say, "knocked silly" by what they "saw." They may suddenly have seen something quite mundane—but seen it clearly—such as the insanity of a world in which masses of foodstuffs are being destroyed when millions of men and women go hungry. An artist may see a beauty of line or light that leaves him almost fainting, and causes him to regard what he has painted—once he is forced to twist his mind back to it—with a sick disgust. All that St. Thomas Aquinas wrote was of the highest intellectual value or significance: yet, in proportion as he advanced to a more intimate knowledge of God, he wanted to cross it all out.... On a day, I may suddenly see what a caricature of love is lust: what an abomination it is that *I* should scorn my fellow-man, whatever his limitations; or a simple truth, such as that some day I shall die; or a sublime one, such as that God exists; or, that He loves me; or even, that Christ really was crucified, and what this meant; or again, how all but infinitely different my life as a baptised, exempted Christian is, or as a priest is, from what it could have been and therefore should have been. What I could never put into words: what I could never sufficiently formulate in ideas (for the ideas have been familiar to me ever since I learnt my catechism; and I have no *new* words nor grouping of words, in which to say anything whatsoever). The mists have parted; trumpets have sounded; light has been poured forth as from a bowl. My life has been shaken to its foundations at a mere moment's contact with Reality. I go staggering for a day at a time under this frightful but glorious undecipherable shock; I know only that it *has been* administered; any attempt on *my* part to reconstruct it lands me only in imitations and pretences; very soon I can hardly see what any of it meant; I retain a notion that now seems obvious and then seemed more mysterious, more exalting, than the human heart might conceive—that "I can serve God," for example: that "Jesus Christ was truly man"; that I am "redeemed." Well, I need not be so terribly upset—St. Teresa herself said that soon enough after her revelations she could hardly believe that she had ever had them. But, a long way short of revelations, we can and do see thus clearly what after a moment or two means next to nothing to us, smothered as we are by our normal bodily experiences, all concerned, on their own level, with appearances and not with reality, nor with the value of reality, at all.

Think then, for a moment, what it must be to find oneself without a body! Nothing but a mind left, able to see what is really real, and what matters, and how intensely it matters—and mattered even when it seemed to me of no particular importance. Herein, I should say—even apart from any partial vision of Himself that may then be accorded to us—is the preliminary anguish of Purgatory. I see, what never now I see, what Fact is, what Reality is. I am stripped of the manifold illusions generated by the senses. I see fact in perspective; I see its value; and I see it with an intensity tolerable only because God supports me. Pray often, pray with all that is in you—that is, pray calmly in reliance on the grace of Christ that is in you, on Christ who is in you and the Spirit within your spirit—for the Souls in Purgatory who are enduring (and, even as you pray, are some of them beginning—or nearly ceasing—to endure) that vision so probing that it goes between the bone and the marrow, the reasoning mind itself and the contemplating spirit! At the lowest, think what will be your own alleviation, in that hour, if you have myriads of souls praying for you out of gratitude that you once helped them in *their* hour. Imagination will not help you here; for you will be seeing what is at least as much disguised, now, by imagination, as rendered accessible to you by means of any picturings.

Now you can begin to assess the rapture of Mary who forthwith after her death started to contemplate what even she, on earth, had seen but "as by means of a mirror, dimly." At least she had no distorted image to rectify; she had worshipped no idol; the world's vast cheat had never illusioned her. Such mirror as there had been had been her whole

self—*Speculum Iustitiae*: all that was right, and only that, had been reflected in her. Even when she realised that she had never conceived
what the eternal Truth and Beauty and Love really were, she had not
to say, as we shall have to: "I conceived them awry; I conceived them
with immeasurably less clarity than I *could* have done; I withdrew my
love even from what I did see." She could say: "The hundredth part was
not told me! What I saw was true. Yet not even I was *able* to see that it
was really *this*! What I loved, I rightly loved and I never loved anything
at its expense. And, therefore, I find that I can love, and am loving, and
am united with, what surpasses—beyond all calculation—all that even
I had known of lovableness!" Our souls, in Purgatory, will have a joy
almost as intolerable as their sorrow: for we shall know that we are safe,
that we are becoming momentarily more able to see and love that which
alone is Holy and Supreme. But she could have the joy without any of
the backward anguish.

We have now but to add that it should not be hard for us to *understand* the immense access of joy that will be ours when we are fully
because of completion reformed according to our true nature. I say: "understand," and should, better, have continued, "*that* the access of joy will
be immense when we are once more, and perfectly, body-soul." For it
stands to reason that we cannot properly *imagine* what it will be like to
be glorified in body and in soul. It is precisely what the eye hath *not* seen,
what the ear hath *not* heard, what it has not so much as entered into the
heart of man to conceive—says St. Paul—that God has prepared in the
way of good things for them that love Him. We can build up our imagi-
native pictures out of such material as is now at our disposal—fancying
how the eye should supply us with nothing save what is most beautiful,
the ear with what is wholly harmonious; how instinct and intelligence

shall be no more in rivalry, nor the will ever flag; and how we could be always at the very peak of our appreciation of what is good: but this is only a sort of exaggerating the best we now experience, according to amount: our experience *then* will be something better also in kind. Still, we can understand the *fact,* and look forward to it.

But today we are prepared to forget ourselves for the sake of Our Lady in whose glorification we wish to rejoice, as do the Angels. *Assumpta est Maria in caelum—Gaudent Angeli!* The Liturgy keeps putting those words upon our lips during this Octave. And observe both parts of that sentence. The joy of the Angels at any rate is quite disinterested. It was not they who were redeemed by the Sacrifice of Him who was Mary's Son. It is, in a sense, and so far as we know, more than disinterested; it is a self-humbling joy, inasmuch as they see that God has done greater things for Man who, by nature, is below themselves. In the hierarchy of being, those pure spirits are more exalted than our human nature is, so mixed and enigmatical. Yet *exaltata est sancta Dei Genetrix super choros angelorum*—high above those angels has human nature, and not only part of it—the part that corresponds, so to say, to the angels—been uplifted. True, they had already contemplated the Incarnation Glorified; but, speaking as best we can, in our limited way, "God was in Christ," reconciling the world to Himself; nay, "the Word *was* God." It would indeed have been strange if He of His own power had not carried that human nature that He had assumed right up both in body and in soul into glory. But Mary had not thus the very source of life within herself. Great things were done *to* her and *for* her; but *for* her and *unto* her they all of them were done. This is why the Angels, on beholding the glorification of Mary, rejoice, as we do, and forthwith, as we must, turn to God to thank Him and to praise Him.

RICHARD CRASHAW

⚘ ⚘

ON THE GLORIOUS ASSUMPTION
OF OUR BLESSED LADY

Hark! she is call'd, the parting houre is come
Take thy Farewell, poor world! heav'n must goe home
A piece of heav'nly earth; purer and brighter
Than the chaste stars, whose choice lamps come to light her
While through the crystall orbes, clearer than they
She climbes; and makes a far more milky way.
She's call'd. Hark, how the dear immortall dove
Sighes to his silver mate, rise up, my love!
Rise up, my fair, my spotlesse one!
The winter's past, the rain is gone.

　　The Spring is come, the flow'rs àppear
No sweets, but thou, are wanting here.
　　Come away, my love!
　　Come away, my dove! cast off delay,
　　The court of heav'n is come
　　To wait upon thee home;
　　Come come away!

The flow'rs appear,
Or quickly would, wert thou once here.
The spring is come, or if it stay,
'Tis to keep time with thy delay.
The rain is gone, except so much as we
Detain in needful teares to weep the want of thee.
   The winter's past.
   Or if he make lesse haste,
His answer is, why, she does so.
If summer come not, how can winter goe.
   Come away, come away.
The shrill winds chide, the waters weep thy stay;
The fountains murmur; and each loftiest tree
Bowes low'st his heavy top, to look for thee.
   Come away, my love.
   Come away, my dove, &c.
She's call'd again. And will she goe?
When heav'n bids come, who can say no?
Heav'n calls her, and she must away.
Heav'n will not, and she cannot stay.
Goe then; goe Glorious.
   On the golden wings
Of the bright youth of heav'n, that sings
Under so sweet a Burthen, Goe,
Since thy dread son will have it so.
And while thou goest, our song and we
Will, as we may, reach after thee.
Hail, holy Queen of humble hearts!

We in thy praise will have our parts.
   Thy pretious Name shall be
   Thy self to us; and we
   With holy care will keep it by us.
   We to the last
   Will hold it fast
   And no Assumption shall deny us.
   All the sweetest show'res
   Of our fairest flow'res
   Will we strow upon it.
   Though our sweets cannot make
   It sweeter, they can take
   Themselves new sweetness from it.
Maria, men and Angels sing
Maria, mother of our King.

   Live, rosy princesse. Live. And may the bright
Crown of a most incomparable light
Embrace thy radiant browes. O may the best
Of everlasting joyes bathe thy white breast.
Live, our chast love, the holy mirth
Of heav'n; the humble pride of earth.
Live, crown of women; Queen of men.
Live mistresse of our song. And when
Our weak desires have done their best,
Sweet Angels come, and sing the rest.

᪣ ᪣

THE CORONATION

Our Lady, in the order of nature, is lower in the scale of being than the angels. But in the order of grace she is higher than they. No creation of God has ever approached her greatness, her perfection, her closeness to her Creator. This mystery is not merely that she becomes Queen of Heaven because Christ crowns her, but rather that He crowns her because she is already Queen.

Chesterton, hundreds of years later, was fascinated by the thought of a woman crowned queen of the angelic host. Man has been made "a little lower than the angels"; yet the Son of Man, who is God, had a human mother, and her the angels worship. Yet still she is *ours*, he boasted as he wrote:

> *Our Lady went into a strange country,*
> *Our Lady, for she was ours*
> *And had run on the little hills behind the houses*
> *And pulled small flowers;*
> *But she rose up and went into a strange country*
> *With strange thrones and powers.*

Our Lady went into a strange country
And they crowned her for a queen,
For she needed never to be stayed or questioned
But only seen;
And they were broken down under unbearable beauty
As we have been.

Our Lady wears a crown in a strange country
The crown He gave,
But she has not forgotten to call her old companions,
To call and crave;
And to hear her calling a man might arise and thunder
On the doors of the grave.

Our Lady is the one complete human person in heaven. There are many human souls—the saints—but they will only be complete as persons when at the Last Day they get their bodies again. Our Lord took to heaven a complete human nature, but His is the Person of God the Son. Mary alone is a human person in heaven, body and soul: a complete human person, crowned by her Son Queen of the angels and saints and Queen of men.

G. K. CHESTERTON

THE TRINKETS

A wandering world of rivers,
    A wavering world of trees,
If the world grow dim and dizzy
    With all changes and degrees,
It is but Our Lady's mirror
    Hung dreaming in its place,
Shining with only shadows
    Till she wakes it with her face.

The standing whirlpool of the stars,
    The wheel of all the world,
Is a ring on Our Lady's finger
    With the suns and moons empearled,
With stars for stones to please her
    Who sits playing with her rings
With the great heart that a woman has
    And the love of little things.

THE BOOK OF THE BLESSED VIRGIN

Wings of the whirlwind of the world
  From here to Ispahan,
Spuming the flying forests,
  Are light as Our Lady's fan:
For all things violent here and vain
  Lie open and all at ease
Where God has girded Heaven to guard
  Her holy vanities.

SOURCES OF THE SELECTIONS

Father Martindale's from *Our Blessed Lady.*

Maurice Zundel's from *Our Lady of Wisdom.*

Charles Journet's from *Our Lady of Sorrows.*

Fr. Leen's from *In the Likeness of Christ.*

Fr. Vincent McNabb's from *New Testament Witness to Our Lady.*

Maisie Ward's from *The Splendor of the Rosary.*

Hilaire Belloc's from *Sonnets and Verse.*

Caryll Houselander's prose from *The Reed of God* and poems from *The Flowering Tree.*

G. K. Chesterton's poems from *The Queen of Seven Swords.*

THE BOOK OF THE BLESSED VIRGIN

F. J. Sheed's from *Theology and Sanity*.

Msgr. Knox's from *A Retreat for Priests*.

Sister Maris Stella's from *Frost for St. Brigid*.

Paul Claudel's from *Ways and Crossways*.

Sigrid Undset's from *Christmas and Twelfth Night*.

Dietrich von Hildebrand's from In *Defense of Purity*.

The translations of the old English poems on p. 89 and p. 129 are by Margaret Williams, R.S.C.J. They appear in her *Wordhoard*.

The translation of the Boccaccio sonnet is by Francis MacManus. It is in his *Boccaccio*.

Poems not included in the above list will be found in *Poetry and Life*, an Anthology.

Designed by Fiona Cecile Clarke, the CLUNY MEDIA *logo*
depicts a monk at work in the scriptorium,
with a cat sitting at his feet.

The monk represents our mission to emulate
the invaluable contributions of the monks
of Cluny in preserving the libraries of the West,
our strivings to know and love the truth.

The cat at the monk's feet is Pangur Bán, from the
eponymous Irish poem of the 9th century.
The anonymous poet compares his scholarly
pursuit of truth with the cat's happy hunting of mice.
The depiction of Pangur Bán is an homage to the work
of the monks of Irish monasteries and a sign
of the joy we at Cluny take in our trade.

"Messe ocus Pangur Bán,
cechtar nathar fria saindan:
bíth a menmasam fri seilgg,
mu memna céin im saincheirdd."

Made in the USA
Middletown, DE
19 February 2024

49680879R00149